STUDIES IN ENGLISH LITERATURE No. 37

General Editor

David Daiches

Professor of English in the School of English and
American Studies, University of Sussex

T. S. ELIOT:
THE WASTE LAND

by

HELEN WILLIAMS

Lecturer in English Literature,
University of Edinburgh

EDWARD ARNOLD

© HELEN WILLIAMS 1973

First published 1968 by
Edward Arnold (Publishers) Ltd.,
25 Hill Street, London W1X 8LL

Second edition 1973

Cloth edition ISBN: 0 7131 5674 0

Paper edition ISBN: 0 7131 5675 9

*Printed offset in Great Britain by
The Camelot Press Ltd., London and Southampton*

General Preface

It has been increasingly clear in recent years that what both the advanced sixth-former and the university student need most by way of help in their literary studies are close critical analyses and evaluations of individual works. Generalisations about periods or authors, general chat about the Augustan Age or the Romantic Movement, have their uses; but often they provide merely the illusion of knowledge and understanding of literature. All too often students come up to the university under the impression that what is required of them in their English literature courses is the referring of particular works to the appropriate generalisations about the writer or his period. Without taking up the anti-historical position of some of the American 'New Critics', we can nevertheless recognise the need for critical studies that concentrate on the work of literary art rather than on its historical background or cultural environment.

The present series is therefore designed to provide studies of individual plays, novels and groups of poems and essays, which are known to be widely studied in sixth forms and in universities. The emphasis is on clarification and evaluation; biographical and historical facts, while they may of course be referred to as helpful to an understanding of particular elements in a writer's work, will be subordinated to critical discussion. What kind of work is this? What exactly goes on here? How good is the work and why? These are questions which each writer will try to answer.

DAVID DAICHES

Contents

Introductory

It needs more than T. S. Eliot's own belief that every generation must make a poem in its own image to justify adding to the number of interpretations of *The Waste Land*. We may, however, agree with the writer in *The Times Literary Supplement*, September 28, 1962, that 'There is no general agreement about what kind of poem *The Waste Land* is', so this does seem a good moment to offer an estimate of its permanent importance and to analyse precisely the kind of demands it makes upon readers. There will always be those who agree with Wyndham Lewis who in *Man Without Art* (1934) called the poem 'this cross-word puzzle of synthetic literary chronology, of spurious verbal algebra', and whilst source-hunters[1] have provided a great *Road to Xanadu* for *The Waste Land*, this kind of help can be difficult to use. There is a danger of the reader's experience of the whole poem becoming fragmented into a disconnected collection of familiar and unknown quotations which, when reassembled. do not seem to correspond to or confirm his original response to the text. The information is valuable, but there is a real lack of direction on how to use it as part of the reading process. Though we may agree with F. R. Leavis, whose influential essay in *New Bearings* (1932) stated that the poem's techniques of 'seeming disjointedness' and allusiveness 'reflect the present state of civilisation' with its 'irrevocable loss of that sense of absoluteness which seems necessary to a robust culture', the poem can no longer be important to us if it is merely an evocation of the *malaise* of the early twenties.

In *Thoughts after Lambeth* (1931)[2] Eliot himself disclaimed that praise of his poem which so stressed his particular generation: 'I may have expressed for them their own illusion of being disillusioned, but that did not form part of my intention'. What was his intention can never be absolutely established, nor should a poet's known intention blind us to defects in the poetic realisation of that intention in the finished work. He remarked in *Tradition and Experiment*, an address delivered at the City

---

[1] G. Williamson, *A Reader's Guide to T. S. Eliot* (New York, 1953); G. Grover Smith, *T. S. Eliot's Poetry and Plays: A Study in Sources and Meanings* (Chicago, 1956).

[2] For this and all references to Eliot's critical essays in the text, see list on p. 96.

Library, Oxford, 1929, that 'The current superstition that our epoch is Alexandrine, decadent, or disillusioned is parallel; there are no "disillusioned" ages, only disillusioned individuals; and our time is just as deluded as any other.' Eliot, with his prevailing interest in time, and his attempt, under the influence of F. H. Bradley, to see the present not merely as ephemeral but as an illusory state since it actually embodies both our past and future, tried in his poem to place the particular experience of his own generation in a context beyond time. There it would be distanced and its significance seen in permanent terms. Such a transcendence of the temporary should be reflected in the poet's method; he would try, in fact, to use the 'historical sense', and such a 'sense', such a possession of 'tradition' could be articulated by the incorporation in the new poem of many echoes and elements of our whole literature; by the famous technique of allusion. But allusion should not result merely in a patchwork of quotations, of past idioms, nor in poetry of a cold impersonality which the chemical metaphors used in *Tradition and the Individual Talent* might suggest. With T. E. Hulme, who in *Speculations* spoke of the poet getting 'the exact curve of what he sees, object or idea', and Pound who described poetry as 'a sort of inspired mathematics, which gives us equations . . . for human emotions', the Eliot of the twenties saw poetry as the making of objects rather than the communication of the artist's personality to others. Whatever of the poet's personal emotions survive in the poem, should do so in a changed, objectified form which Eliot recurrently expresses in the metaphor, drawn from Shakespeare's *The Tempest*, of the *sea-change* which permeates his poems and criticism. Although the reader's experience will then be primarily aesthetic, and the poet too, in order to give readers such experience, will have had to transmute personal feelings into something outside himself, to Eliot the impersonality of art is in no way synonymous with inhumanity or abstraction. Its intensity should perhaps be white rather than red-hot.

So it is with the form and patterning of material in *The Waste Land* that I want to deal, rather than with the nature of the material itself or the significance of the emotion generated. These have been discussed, perhaps to excess. Patterning can be examined in two aspects of the poem: in its form which startled many early critics and is still sometimes considered to be a pseudo-form betraying real failure to organise material, and in the technique of allusion which has been admired or decried but rarely closely analysed as a way of writing.

1. Pattern as Form

I

The common end of all *narrative*, nay, of *all* Poems, is to convert a series into a whole: to make those events, which in real or imagined History move on in a strait line, assume to our understandings a circular motion—the snake with its tail in its mouth.
Collected Letters of S. T. Coleridge, ed. E. L. Griggs, Vol. II (1959), p. 218

When in *Tradition and the Individual Talent* Eliot speaks of a separation taking place between the man who suffers and the mind that creates, it has often been too hastily assumed that he is suggesting the total irrelevance to the artistic process of the human capacity to suffer and feel. Rather, Eliot uses the word 'suffering' in strict antithesis to 'creating', stressing the sense of passivity, of endurance, in the word, using it within a context of artistic activity rather than in a general context of life versus art. At an early stage in composition, this state of receptivity may provide the mind of the artist with its store of heterodox material (such as the famous example in 'Metaphysical Poets' of reading Spinoza, being in love and cooking) but it must not afterwards interfere in the active selection and shaping of material. This active, shaping faculty is concerned primarily with the choice of the significant and the rejection of the merely personal from the demanding particulars which may all be equally important to the personality. In his introduction to a translation of Paul Valéry's *Le Serpent* in 1924, Eliot clarifies his ideas on the relations between personality and art, outlined only suggestively in *Tradition and the Individual Talent*. The surrender of personality to art or to a system of ideas is itself, he says, a 'passionate act', not an arid turning from life. Emotions, experiences and ideas are of course retained in art, but transmuted, for:

> one is prepared for art when one has ceased to be interested in one's own emotions and experiences except as material and when one has reached this point of indifference one will pick and choose according to very different principles from those who are still excited by their own feelings.

It is the pattern which expresses the significant relations between particulars in a poem that becomes its original element. The pattern may be as new to 'the man who suffers' as to the reader, but not to the conscious mind of the creating artist.

Eliot's interest in the organisation of material comes out remarkably in the two *London Letters* written for *The Dial* in July and October 1921, a period during which he was at work on *The Waste Land*. The description of London's atmosphere itself bears curious resemblances to details of the poem and to the irony which plays in it.

'The vacant term of wit set in early this year with a fine, hot, rainless spring; the crop of murders and divorces has been poor compared with that of last autumn.' So we have the 'cruellest month' and a hint of Stetson and Lil. He describes too a form of influenza which 'leaves extreme dryness and a bitter taste in the mouth'. The fine weather has revealed in its 'blazing glare' 'towers and steeples of uncontaminated white', which surprise in their murky setting as do the 'white towers' in the sweating river passage in the unreal city of 'The Fire Sermon'. A journalistic lament that the opera has fled to New York takes on for a moment the 'Waste Land' tone, for the opera had been 'one of the last reminders of a former excellence of life, a sustaining symbol even for those who seldom went'. Wagner opera becomes, indeed, a 'sustaining symbol' in the poem.†
These details may be accidental but when he comes to his main subject, Diaghilev's New Ballet, the concern with making a form out of particulars takes us straight into Eliot's poetic workshop. The New Ballet, he says, is both more sophisticated and simpler than the old, and 'what is needed of art is a simplification of current life into something rich and strange'. Here again the favourite *Tempest* metaphor is used to suggest making something fixed from the flux of the transient. The stress upon a blend of sophistication with simplicity makes it clear that what he elsewhere claims to be the necessary difficulty of modern art does not lie merely in a chaotic multiplicity of material. Art must do more than mirror or express the complexity of experience.

The same interests are evident in the October letter, when he reviewed Stravinsky's *Rite of Spring* which had scandalised Paris audiences in 1913 just as Joyce's *Ulysses* was now causing a censorship scandal. What excited Eliot in the piece was its attempted fusion of modernity with primitive ritual, a fusion akin to his own attempt to unite the worlds of Lil and the 'young man carbuncular' with that of the Fisher King and the Grail Knights and maidens in his poem. In the total work Eliot felt such fusion was not achieved: 'The spirit of the music was modern and the spirit of the ballet was primitive ceremony.' Thus, however interesting

† refers to the Appendix, pp. 76–7.

the work might be to readers like himself of Frazer's *The Golden Bough*, as a whole it failed to achieve that 'interpenetration and metamorphosis' necessary to art. It was only Stravinsky's music that conveyed a sense of the present, fusing ancient and modern in its idiom. The ballet was only a pseudo-historic articulation of an ancient rite, while the music 'did seem to transform the rhythm of the Steppes into the scream of the motor horns . . . and the barbaric cries of modern life . . . into music'.[3]† Interestingly he suggests that the use of anthropological material would not in itself guarantee that fusion. *The Golden Bough* or, presumably Jessie L. Weston's book *From Ritual to Romance* can either be read as history in the dead sense of information about the past in 'a collection of entertaining myths' or as history in a living sense of tradition, that is, as a 'revelation of that vanished mind of which our mind is a continuation'. So Eliot is already seeing myth and ritual here as a potential means of ordering and transforming into significance, contemporary experience. Their technical function seems to have been even more important to him than their symbolic meaning.

By November 1923, after *The Waste Land*'s publication, Eliot is even more explicit about this problem. The very title of his review in *The Dial* of Joyce's *Ulysses* makes the point—*Ulysses, Order and Myth*. He sets out to answer the challenge of readers who, in terms used by many early readers of *The Waste Land*, saw *Ulysses* as 'an invitation to chaos; an expression of feelings which are perverse, partial and a distortion of reality'. Eliot, in answer to this, calls the work *classical* and complains that people have underestimated the importance of the *Odyssey* parallel as a structural device: 'In using the myth, in manipulating a continuous parallel between contemporaneity and antiquity, Mr. Joyce is pursuing a method which others must pursue after him.' Then comes the famous remark which sounds so like a comment on his own *The Waste Land*: 'It is simply a way of controlling and ordering, of giving a shape and a significance to the immense panorama of futility and anarchy which is contemporary history.' Eliot's own technique for presenting the 'immense panorama' is different from Joyce's. By compression and allusion he condenses it where Joyce expands the moment almost to infinitude, but both resort to a back-cloth of mythology to hold their material in a shape.

But it would be facile to suppose that the use of mythological parallells in a work which is superficially about a contemporary situation will

[3] Eliot was clearly not impressed by the choreography of Leonide Massine, which had replaced that of Nijinsky.

automatically guarantee either artistic form or the work's permanent importance, saving it from the fate of topical satire: from fashion. Looking back we can already see that the use of myth and the then recent discovery of its supposed anthropological roots and psychological implications was itself one of the great fashions of the twenties.* In particular, the American 'exiles' (Gertrude Stein's 'Lost Generation') in Paris sought to stiffen their work by myth. A common theme in Eliot and in this group was the problem of retaining fertility and spiritual awareness within the context of modern civilisation. This may well be one of the most modish aspects of *The Waste Land* when the poem is looked at in a context of literary history. Moreover, in using material from Frazer's cultivation rituals and Jessie L. Weston's Fisher King and Grail myths, Eliot is taking over something far too complex to provide his poem with a 'continuous parallel' or shadow-hero of the journey-shaped narrative kind provided by the *Odyssey*. The structure which they provide behind the cluttered 'proscenium of modern life' in Eliot's *Waste Land* is almost as intricate as the proscenium itself. The thematic contribution of the Fisher King legend is familiar/the Fisher King has lost his virility through sexual mutilation (i.e. maiming) or sickness and this is associated with the desolation of his lands. Crops cannot grow and the power of propagation is suspended. The curse of aridity can only be removed by a quester, a youthful knight who must undertake the journey to the castle or chapel of the Grail, submit to trial, ascertain the office of the Grail and the significance of the symbols of lance and cup. If he succeeds the King will be healed and the land restored to fertility. The Christian symbolism of the cup and lance, the lance which pierced Christ's side and the cup or chalice used at the Last Supper and preserved by Joseph of Arimathea to receive some

---

* For an interesting observation of this trend, see Adams, R. P., 'Sunrise out of The Waste Land' *Tulane Studies in English* (IX, 1959), pp. 119–31.

The following chronology may also be of interest:

January 1922, Ernest Hemingway established residence in Paris and met Pound.

February 1922, James Joyce's *Ulysses* published in Paris.

October 1922, T. S. Eliot's *The Waste Land* published in *Criterion* I, 1.

October 1922, article by V. Larbaud on the Odyssey parallels in Joyce's *Ulysses* in *Criterion* I, 1.

November 1923, Eliot, 'Ulysses, Order and Myth', *Dial* (LXXV, 5).

April 1925, Scott Fitzgerald, *The Great Gatsby* published and sent to T. S. Eliot.

May 1925, Scott Fitzgerald arrived in Paris.

of Christ's blood at the crucifixion is linked with pagan prece-
dents. Here cup and lance are female and male sex symbols and the fertility gods, Adonis, Attis and Osiris are associated with red or purple
flowers symbolising the sacrificial flow of their blood to fertilise the land.
There is a relic of this symbolism in the two red suits in the modern pack
of cards, the diamond being the lance head and the heart the chalice.

But Eliot, in admitting a debt to Jessie L. Weston, is acknowledging
something more complicated than a mythological source for his themes.
Jessie L. Weston posits a complex synthesis both historical and geographical behind the twelfth-century medieval Grail legends. Her major
claim is that 'in the Grail King we have a romantic literary version of
that strange mysterious figure whose presence hovers in the shadowy
background of the history of our Aryan race; the figure of a divine or
semi-divine ruler, at once god and king, upon whose life, and unim-
paired vitality, the existence of his land and people directly depends.'
The common element in all forms of the myth is the 'affirmation of life
and the rejuvenation of the Vegetation God' frequently symbolised
by the 'freeing of the waters'. She traces the life-cult back from its
Christianised form in the Grail legends, where the redeeming of the
land from barrenness has spiritual as well as natural implications, through
its 'fully evolved classical form . . . the cult of Adonis' to 'fragmentary
relics of Aryan and Babylonian antiquity'. From twelfth-century
Romance Europe she moves back to the Phoenician-Greek Adonis,
whose cults were recorded as early as 700 B.C., to Sumerian-Babylonian
Tammuz who can be traced to 3000 B.C., and to the nature-ritual dramas
of the thousand poems of the Hindu *Rig-Veda* of 'our Aryan forefathers'.
Her acknowledged debt to Frazer expands even further the tracing
across time and space of the common basis of a vegetation life cult. In
bringing the literary Grail material (positing, for example a sexual
symbolism for the Grail cup and lance and a feast-of-life origin for the
Eucharist) into the realm of anthropology, Jessie L. Weston crosses the
frontiers between history and legend, science and conjecture which
might make the book suspect to a professional anthropologist but
exciting to a poet. When, in his note, Eliot claims that 'not only the
title, but the plan and a good deal of the incidental symbolism' are
derived from the book, he is acknowledging a debt in this attempt to
synthesise time and space by analysis of the persisting common elements
in myth. This has the effect of neutralising local and temporal differences. This is again a debt to method, for, as he later shows by the

scornful way he dismisses those whom his Notes sent on a goose-chase after the Grail,[4] the themes and symbols borrowed are clear and obvious and can be recognised on a very small knowledge of Frazer or Weston.

It clearly fitted part of Eliot's poetic intention to cast his vision of a contemporary predicament, one of natural, erotic and spiritual aridity, into a general perspective beyond barriers of historical time or national or geographical boundaries. Miss Weston's thesis contributes to this theme because it links natural and often erotically expressed cults with a spiritual quest for fulfilment, in the notion of higher and lower planes of initiation. But as an ordering device, her contribution is complicated. How can this cluster of myth and legend become a controlling factor in the poem? Do we have to re-awaken a belief in these myths, or even an I. A. Richards' pseudo-faith in them, to get the point of the parallels Eliot is drawing? In his comments upon *Ulysses* and *The Rite of Spring* we can see that he is excited by other artists' use of myth and anthropology *not* primarily because of what this material says or means in itself. (This can be interesting, but like ideas or systems of belief, should not 'possess' the artist.) It is as a technical device that he appreciates them.

It is not at first easy to see what kind of shape and structure the vegetation and Grail myths give to *The Waste Land*. As F. R. Leavis wrote in *New Bearings in English Poetry* (1932) 'a poem that is to contain all myths cannot construct itself upon one.' But one may be reluctant to agree with his further claim that comprehensiveness is gained at the cost of structure or with Conrad Aiken who thought that '*The Waste Land* material is merely a superficial binding net to contain, if not unify the poem's ideas.'[5] Both sets of myth, Eliot believed with Miss Weston, were rooted in the seasonal cycle and its recurrent rhythms. This is perhaps why, whatever order this material bestows on the poem, it is not that of a point by point, episodic, narrative parallel. Critics who complain of the poem's lack of structure have perhaps been too bent on discovering in it a narrative form, events set in time. It is unfortunate that I. A. Richards' impressive phrase 'condensed epic' has been taken technically as the name of a basically narrative shape, not qualitatively, as was surely intended, to suggest the weight and importance of the content invoked by Eliot's method of allusion. Many critics have proceeded as if the shape of this 'condensed epic' of 434 lines were narrative, episodes set in order but with the connecting links and conventional development of heroic character suppressed to achieve poetic economy (such a supposition lies behind Yvor Winters' complaint of a 'non-existent plot and people denoted by acts which are not arranged in narrative'[6]); too often the main business of the critic has become the supply of these missing links, the offering of a logical or narrative structure in place of the poem. The favourite cinematic label given to Eliot's technique has too often led to the poem's being discussed as a trailer to a missing 'big film'.

II

If we think of a scale of structures having at one end logic, the completely reasoned and abstracted, and at the other some form of madness or surrealism, matter or impression unformed and undisciplined (the imitation of disorder by the idiom of disorder), we may see metaphysical and neoclassical poetry as near the extreme of logic . . . and romantic poetry as a step toward the directness of Sensory presentation. . . . The romantic is far closer than the metaphysical to symbolist poetry and the varieties of postsymbolist most in vogue today.

From W. K. Wimsatt, *The Verbal Icon* (University of Kentucky Press, 1954), p. 116

There is still no evidence that even before Ezra Pound's notorious Caesarian operation upon the poem, when he cut episodes and changed the order of the remaining parts, its shape was a linear narrative in disguise. Pound was one of the first to connect the cinematographic metaphor with art based on urban material. In an article for *The Dial* for 1922 he drew a distinction which illuminates discussion of the non-narrative form of Eliot's poem of projected city and desert. 'The life of the village is narrative; you have not been there three weeks before you know [the whole story]. . . . In a city the visual impressions succeed each other, overlap, overcross, they are cinematographic.' Eliot's 'unreal city' is of course a topos, not merely a place. The city *is* its swarming life. As Shakespeare makes a citizen ask of Rome in *Coriolanus*,[7] the

[6] Y. Winters, 'T. S. Eliot or, The Illusion of Reaction', essay in *The Anatomy of Nonsense* (Norfolk, New Directions, 1943), pp. 460–501.
[7] III i. 198.

play so admired and used by Eliot, 'What is the city but the people.'
Eliot himself, in his London letter written for *The Dial* in April 1922,
describes London's human and literary atmosphere as one of moral
cowardice rooted, he felt, in chauvinistic provincialism; hence, 'other
cities decay; London merely shrivels, like a little book-keeper grown
old'. Taken together, these extracts from the poet and his 'miglior
fabbro' suggest a link between the emotional content, with its urban
symbolisation, and the discontinuous *form* of *The Waste Land*. Having
manipulated his Grail sources and his oriental allusions, and having, as
he declared in his Notes, attempted a 'collocation of eastern and western
asceticism', Eliot must also have been alerted by an article in *The Dial*
for January that same year, '*Oriental Dances in America*'. Ananda
Coomaraswamy, an oriental observer of western cultural malaise,
aware of a 'cult' of oriental imitation in western art, shrewdly remarks
that 'The chaotic character of modern western art is the symptom of its
lack of inner necessity'; and concludes, 'An ancient art may be a source
of inspiration, it may guide us in matters of principle—since beauty is
independent of time and place—but, it ought not to be regarded as a
model for our imitation.'

For all his use of oriental allusion in The Fire Sermon and the commands of The Thunder God, Eliot does not attempt any formal imitation
in this sense, but neither does he surrender entirely to deliberate expres-
sive formlessness. He attempts rather a sequence of concentrated and
intense impressions ordered according to a 'logic of the imagination'.
The very willingness to accept changes of length and order of episodes
shows how little Eliot was thinking in terms of narrative or logical
forms. If we move to the other extreme and suggest that the connection
between episodes is entirely arbitrary, a deliberate chaos reflecting chaos,
we are dangerously near being forced to accept Winters' accusation of
the 'fallacy of imitative form'. Before agreeing with Paul Elmer More[8]
that Eliot is a 'lyric prophet of chaos', one should remember Eliot's
notion of a 'logic of the imagination'. Winters believed that 'You need
to be clearly in control of the confusion you wish to express', and
thought Eliot lacked this control because he had felt obliged to 'seek his
form in his matter'. Where Baudelaire achieved control over his subject,
Eliot surrenders to it. Since Eliot was himself a great champion of

[8] P. E. More, review in *The Saturday Review of Literature* (1932), quoted
in L. Unger ed., *T. S. Eliot: a Selected Critique* (New York, 1948), pp. 24–9.

Baudelaire, both as a poet and prose writer, it may be appropriate to cite Baudelaire's definition of Imagination:[9]

> It decomposes all of creation, and, with the materials gathered, set forth according to rules whose origin cannot be found except in the deepest part of the soul, it creates a new world, and produces the experience of the new.

This Coleridgean definition with its appeal to the 'deepest part of the soul' is essentially Romantic, admitting the importance of a sub or super-rational intervention in the creative process. But it also speaks of rules and the creation of a new order and does not suggest the random imitation or reflecting of 'decomposed' experience. This is where order and Eliot's 'logic of the imagination' may come in. There is controlling art behind apparent fragmentation.

The real test of Winters' attack can only be an analysis of the poem itself in terms of its odd structure. The reader must decide for himself whether having, at some stage, submerged himself in 'the destructive element', Eliot remained in it, merely giving it uncontrolled expression, or whether he comes out with a form which is itself some kind of comment or judgement upon his material.*

I approach a description of this structure well aware of I. A. Richards' warning that any intellectual scheme erected by the reader as a way into the poem should merely be scaffolding, 'destined to vanish'. Hence the suggestive character of many former attempts, the cinematic flash, Helen Gardner's spiral in which each ring is a further exploration of the theme, Richards' own 'music of ideas', and F. R. Leavis' development of Eliot's hint of 'an inclusive consciousness'. The Sibyl, prophetess of classical legend, answered questions by throwing from her cave handfuls of leaves containing letters which the person seeking her wisdom was required to arrange into some kind of coherent order. Like the Sibyl, Eliot gives us 'fragments' broken off, dislocated from their contexts: a sequence of scenes, allusions, legendary associations, quotations, and we are left to apprehend their order and meaning. The poem in both its subject and method is a deliberate riddle; here too the epigraph initiates us into a

---

[9] C. Baudelaire, 'La Reine des Facultés', *Salon de 1859* in *Critique d'Art*, éd. Claude Pichois (Paris, 1965), p. 310.

* For an interesting discussion of the relation of Eliot's technique in *The Waste Land* to that of Cubist, Futurist and Surrealist movements in art, see: Jacob Korg, 'Modern Art Techniques in The Waste Land' *Journal of Aesthetics and Art Criticism* (18, 1959–60), pp. 456–63.

B

consistency in Eliot's method. The Sibyl expressed herself in riddles; Tiresias answered Odysseus in a riddle when he descended into hell to question him; Philomel wove her story into a *peplus*; Madame Sosostris, the 'famous clairvoyante', expresses her meaning through the riddle of a 'wicked pack of cards' and the Thunder's tripartite message is a final riddle which draws on the hidden meaning of all the episodes that have gone before. But the 'sibylline leaves' of the poem are not randomly scattered. They have been cast by a directing hand, to form a shape.

The shape of *The Waste Land*, like that of its source myths, is more circular than linear, its order more simultaneous than developing. It is unlike the *Odyssey*, which has a really linear journey-shape, culminating in a return home and the meeting of seeker and sought. The April opening, with its familiar and ironic echoes of a Chaucerian narrative introduction to pilgrimage, may cheat us into expecting a journey with beginning, middle and end. But our conditioned expectations of the season are soon upset: April is cruel, winter kind, because spring stirs the dull roots of growth, memory and desire, inspiring painfully—rather than bringing Chaucer's 'vertue' and 'shoures soote'—the surge of sap which excites. Desire pains and initiative causes fear, not hope. Winter is kind because it buries the half-alive in warmth, 'feeding a little life' but demanding no vital reaction. After such overturning of expectations, we soon realise that the episodes which follow are not to be connected by simple sequence of time or by the logic of cause and effect. Several journeys are undertaken and encounters made, but the main journey, of a protagonist of shifting identity and sex, through the waste land to the chapel is only vestigial as a plot. The very incomplete, fragmentary or anti-climactic nature of these journeys is part of the land's sickness; Marie's journey south in winter to a tourist's Hofgarten, Isolde's two sea journeys, to King Mark and to Tristan and death, the aimless flow of the London crowd, the closed car of the lovers imprisoned in selfhood, the parodic journey which

> brings the sailor home from the sea
> The typist home at tea-time,

Phlebas' terrible journey into decomposition, and the final journey along

> The road winding above among the mountains
> Which are mountains of rock without water

and the allusion, deliberately in hallucinatory form, to the journey to Emmaus. None of these journeys is fulfilled in arrival. We do not even proceed from drought to an Apocalyptic release of rain after an epic struggle across the desert. Instead we begin in a rainy season, and summer surprises Marie, the first protagonist, with 'a shower of rain'. We then proceed alternately through desert, actual or emotional, regions of fire and waters to the agonies of the parching desert in Part V where hallucinations give way, not to climactic relief—'the freeing of the waters'—but to 'the damp gust bringing rain'. The end is the daunting message of the Thunder God, Prajapati, which sounds much more like a challenge to begin again than an end. The Sibylline fragments are gathered at the close but the essential riddle remains unanswered.

This sense of thwarted climax has led to critical dispute about what the ending means. When the protagonist emerges saying:

> I sat upon the shore
> Fishing, with the arid plain behind me

aridity may indeed be behind him but his shoring up of fragments and the setting of the lands in order suggest a preparation for death rather than life, unless it is the necessary death which proceeds spiritual rebirth as in *The Journey of the Magi*. The hinted parallels with Kyd's Hieronymo support this feeling. Argument has centred on whether the quester has come through triumphant, healed by purgation and offering salvation through ascetic withdrawal from sensual life, or whether this end is a final admission of defeat, an ironic dissolving into fragments, a frenetic snatching at random relics of decayed cultures in a crumbling world. Such questions can never, I think, be answered, nor are they the appropriate ones to ask if we abandon the notion of an epic narrative ending for that of a cyclical form. We look then, not for a point of finality, a conclusion hopeful or desperate. The last lines of the poem are quite as ambiguous and paradoxical as its opening. The desert may be crossed but the figure is still fishing. He is moreover fishing in the sea, itself established within the poem as an ambivalent element, being both the source of life, in fish, and of death, in drowning; both the corrosive dissolver of consciousness and yet the agent of the precious sea-change; a cleansing element in which eyes are changed to pearls, earthly sight to vision of great price. As he is still fishing, it seems that the quest for truth, natural if we take the fish as symbol of teeming life, or spiritual if we recall it as ICHTHYS, secret symbol of Christ in the Early Church, is still being undertaken. The offered fragments intensify the ambiguity which forbids our resting in a sense of conclusion, triumphant or nihilistic. Whilst they do seem to drive away the threat of total despair which the hallucinatory visions at the chapel perilous may have engendered, the mood of the last few lines is one of longing, of the reaching after something—'Quando fiam uti chelidon'. When will the poet's voice become that of the swallow, when will he hear or be able to utter its proverbial call—'Console'? Even the recapitulation of the broken images is more complex than the earlier falling towers:

> Jerusalem Athens Alexandria
> Vienna London
> Unreal . . .

The Prince of Aquitaine's tower is fallen like London Bridge, but both could be rebuilt (London Bridge is proverbial for having survived many forms of devastation). There is suggestion of submission to further trial and rebuilding set against the lyrical evocation of cadence in a rhythmic pattern of alternatives. The falling of the bridge is set against the purgatorial fire of Dante where Daniel willingly casts himself back into the refining fire,

> Poi s'ascose nel foco che gli affina.

The 'tour abolie' is set against the longing for transformation into the swallow, sister to the bird of inviolable voice in *A Game of Chess*. The message of Peace emerges from the seeming gibberish of Hieronymo's mad show, delivered in many tongues. The snatches of these tongues which have been used throughout the poem as an image of fragmentation from the bedrock Aryan source are also recapitulated here, but now they are set against Sanskrit words taken from their source tongue. The psychological ruin of madness to both Hamlet and at first to Hieronymo, was itself a deliberate retreat to preserve sanity and justice in an 'upside down' world. The stern commands 'Give, sympathise, control', have all been disobeyed within the poem but they remain as commands, and still promise a consequent peace. 'Shantih' is delivered more in the tone of a promise than of a gift bestowed.

If, then, this ending is more like a new beginning, the circle is here joined up and we have an instance of what Eliot later asserted in *Little Gidding*, V:

And the end of all our exploring
Will be to arrive where we started
And know the place for the first time.

With the retrospective exploration of the poem behind us the way seems bleak, but it is neither nihilistic nor optimistic.

Such a recurrent, cyclical pattern is probably the main formal contribution of the Vegetation and Grail source material to Eliot's poem. Within a circular pattern, itself derived from the revolving of the seasons, the episodes and events compose a simultaneous rather than a developing order, segments in a revolving circle or panels in a medieval altar painting, each individual and with a separate flavour but there as part of a greater and simultaneous whole. Such a breakdown of the tyranny of linear historic time and the logic of cause and effect was perhaps Eliot's great contribution to structure in the twenties.

The nature myth in which the effigy of the dead god is buried or drowned and mourned, to be rediscovered in rejoicing with the release of spring rains, obviously follows a seasonal cycle. The processes of decay and growth and the accompanying emotions of grief and joy are never completed but recur annually. The same pattern of recurrence is also latent in the Grail myths. This may be why, as has often been noted, literary attempts to use the Grail legends resist a straight narrative form. If we accept with Eliot Jessie L. Weston's belief that the Grail legends may have origins in the Nature cycle cults, rather as the Church Year is related to a seasonal calendar so that its festivals incorporate pre-Christian celebrations, the Grail quest can be seen to share the never-ending quality of the seasonal cycle. For this quest is not accomplished once only in historic time and by one particular hero. The achievement is never perfect either for the initiate who cures the sick Fisher King and restores fertility to the land, or for the religious knight searching for a answer to the Grail mysteries. The quest legend being a myth rather than a history can be taken as an emblem for the quest for enlightenment of any soul, a journey like Piers Plowman's search for truth, which has to be undertaken again and again, its true goal being perhaps definable as the will to set out again, even in the face of ruin. The sprouting of the corn-god inevitably heralds its later withering and reburial. The perfect achievement of the Grail would be the bringing of the Kingdom of Heaven on earth and would be apocalyptic in finality. But even in Arthurian legends the forces of destruction soon reassert themselves and the need to take up the quest again recurs.

Since Eliot incorporates these two aspects of his source materials, it is possible to see *The Waste Land* as much as a metaphoric internal landscape of the mind as an external imagistic projection of a dead land. Perceived experience becomes the ego, external and internal meeting in a journey through land or mind: 'our wakeful ego is a perceiving'. This is supported by Eliot's citation in his Notes to the poem of F. H. Bradley's *Appearance and Reality*, where he asserts:

> My external sensations are no less private to myself than are my thoughts or my feelings. In either case my experience falls within my own circle, a circle closed on the outside; and, with all its elements alike, every sphere is opaque to the others which surround it. In brief, regarded as an existence which appears in a soul, the whole world for each is peculiar and private to that soul.

This is not merely an external reference; it is made intrinsic in the sustained imagery of eyes and seeing within the poem. All the paradoxical possibilities of perception, seeing and knowing, earthly and spiritual sight are explored. The subsuming Tiresias, seer though blind, 'can see' and is an instance of the mysterious transformation of eyes into pearls; his loss of earthly sight being compensated by prophetic vision. Similarly the prophet Ezekiel will *show* man fear, through dust, the visible symbol of mortality. The lover in the Hyacinth garden is not the only one whose eyes 'fail'; Madame Sosostris, phoney prophetess, is forbidden to see into mysteries:

> I do not find
> The Hanged man.

The crowd avoid seeing:

> And each man fixed his eyes before his feet.

Belladona's flirtatious Cupidon 'hid his eyes behind his wing', and her own eyes are cheated by the delusions of art so that she cries to her lover:

> You know nothing? Do you see nothing?

and what he remembers is the tag of visual transformation:

> Those are pearls that were his eyes.

The poem's women look vainly or indifferently at their own reflection, seeing nothing:

Her brain allows one half-formed thought to pass

and in the last section, actual sight can no longer be distinguished from what is either vision or hallucination: 'Who is the third who walks always beside you', and the 'doors of perception' are broken as part of a total dissolution of the mind.

The whole 'experience' in the poem then is one man's vision, but contains, through Tiresias' observations, many other more limited apprehensions of reality. The quest may be for an answer to the questions posed by a vision of desolation. Aridity is, after all, the third stage of the traditional mystic's way and this, even to an uncommitted Eliot in 1922, must be one of the many allusions of the desert waste.

If we begin from an underlying patterning of perceived experience as a circle and see the separate episodes and personae as revolving segments, it is clear from the earliest lines of the poem that these two circles are not in harmony and that this is the poem's most important sustained irony. From the moment of the distortion of natural attitudes to season, April cruel and winter kind, we become aware that in developing 'the arts that polish life' man has perverted natural rhythms and can no longer therefore expect a natural restoration of lost vitality, erotic or spiritual. We remember *Gerontion* which Eliot once intended as a Preface to *The Waste Land*:

> I have lost my sight, smell, hearing, taste and touch:
> How should I use them for your closer contact.

In *The Waste Land* the loss of natural vitality is not dependent on old age; it is part of the blight of youth. The quest for rain, symbol of natural growth, is doomed from the beginning in such a world. The river is symbolically polluted by a civilisation whose vitality cannot be restored merely by natural means. The loss of these is hinted in many details; Marie who sheltered from summer rain in the Colonnade and 'reads much of the night' and goes 'south in winter' represents aristocratic boredom and insomnia, perhaps even madness through her connection with the decadent Hapsburgs. Her life pattern reverses day and night, winter and summer. Belladona, too, seeks an anodyne for 'ennui' in the intricacies of chess and among surroundings of high, synthetic artifice. The futility of the quest for rain is, in her case, made explicit. She and her lover reiterate their stale routine:

> The hot water at ten
> And if it rains, a closed car at four.

If the rain falls, they will be protected. Lil's perversion of nature is more drastic. The abortion pills have aged her prematurely and drained her of all vitality. Less extreme, but in the same ironic mode, the typist's food is 'in tins' and her pathetic list of garments suggests shapes which fragment or distort the natural one of the body:

> Stockings, slippers, camisoles, and stays.

The sapped vitality of these inhabitants of the waste, even in its highest and most lyrical form, the lover in the Hyacinth garden who fails and was 'neither living nor dead', places them all in a limbo of the half-alive whose life-cycle can never be harmonised with a natural cycle. Where the two should harmonise they jarr discordantly.

This prevailing disharmony provides the overall framework for the poem's false and true parallels with its source myths, and is therefore one of its means of order and unity. The essential parallel noted by Jessie L. Weston between natural and spiritual vitality, between erotic and religious affirmation, between the lower and higher forms of initiation, is a parallel Eliot believed lost to Western European man not only in twentieth-century London, but in the nearer historic past; it was lost for Goldsmith's lovely lady and Elizabeth I in their stooping to folly, as well as for the typist and her clerk. Behind these, Tristan and Isolde, The Rhine Maidens, Dido and Cleopatra and their lovers had all suffered the same essential loss which lies at the heart of the poem's analysis of human desolation for which the Waste Land itself remains a symbol. This is what Tiresias sees. Through his now detached habit of fore-suffering, he shows it to us in a bleakly reductive form in its contemporary urban version. As the restoration of lost vitality can only now be achieved through transformation, the poem's 'positives' (if one can use so strong a word) all suggest passive endurance, submission, suffering rather than vital activity. Hence the need to apply the word 'epic' to the poem only with very careful reservations.

One of the poetic problems of presenting this theme of lost harmony and vitality is how to present the modern 'reduced' forms of ritual living in anything but a crudely satiric and dismissive way, without, as Alec Brown put it in 1930, 'smartly defining life in its meanest terms'. It has been a common response to the poem, to feel that Eliot is in a Flaubertian tradition, sighing after vanished glories and holding up the present to a cheap and easy scorn. Edwin Muir, for example, a sensitive but uneasy critic, wrote in 1925 that in *The Waste Land* 'an anguished vision of the world is expressed in light verse'.[10] This suggests an essential failure to adjust tone, but tone in the poem's separate episodes is itself governed by the extent to which the reader is willing to take the parallels, real or ironic, with the ground myths and with other episodes which are versions of the common theme. The notorious encounter between the typist and the 'young man carbuncular' (an unfortunate 'Possum' phrase, perhaps) could be thought to show Eliot's too easy ability to expose the urban sordidity which at once repels and fascinates him. Is there cruelty and condescension in the tone which emerges from his *voyeur* stance? Is there even the deep aversion to sexual love which many have attributed to Eliot? The tone of mock-heroic satire, predominant here, runs through the poem. Certainly if one analyses the tone of this segment in isolation, the range of emotions evoked by the encounter may seem narrow. But even in its immediate context there is the complicating factor of the framed observer within the poem, Tiresias, who at this very moment declares his identity and refers to his own bi-sexual nature:

> I Tiresias, though blind, throbbing between two lives,
> Old man with wrinkled female breasts, can see . . .

His tone of prophet's detachment *is* weary, and despite the fact that we might expect the seer to probe beneath surface appearances, he gives us a picture in which local and accidental particulars are all important. For these figures are identified in terms of their possessions and environment, granted no 'character' except in their clumsy and bored gestures and emotions of callow excitement and indifference. Tiresias adds to this bleak vision a historical perspective:

> I who have sat by Thebes below the wall
> And walked among the lowest of the dead.

He recognises an eternal archetype of living death in the scene; to him it is more than a contemporary caricature. He sees too that it is the antithesis of the fertile ecstatic love-encounter which all lovers have sought and which, in the Grail myths, precedes spiritual initiation. But his inward sight gives him a comprehensive despair rather than knowledge which he can use. Ironically, he, and we through him, will recognise

[10] Edwin Muir, 'Contemporary Writers No. III', *Nation and Atheneum* (Aug. 29th, 1925), pp. 644–6.

parallels with the sanctified Grail situation; the lover approaching the hallowed place, met and feasted by a maiden who will be the agent of initiation. There is satiric humour in the portrait of deviation from this ideal, underlined by comic rhymes:

> 'one bold stare'   'millionaire'
> 'as he guesses'   'her in caresses'.

The word 'perilously', loaded in a Grail context, is comically applied to 'her drying combinations'. If this were the only tone at work one might well complain of a lack of compassion. But Eliot in *Appleplex and Eeldrop*, a satiric dialogue written for *The Little Review* in 1917 in which he called himself 'a sceptic, with a taste for mysticism', had claimed that in observing people he sought not to pigeonhole or classify them. One of the results of the decline of orthodox theology, he lamented, was that 'a man is only important as he is classed'. Instead, in observing, he sought and prized 'a moment of unique being, a soul, however insignificant, with a history of its own'. So, here, he suddenly adopts a tone of more sober sadness, again conveyed in flat stark rhythms, but in no way devoid of compassion.

> His vanity requires no response
> And makes a welcome of indifference.

The same act was to be seen in Thebes where Tiresias had seen and foresuffered the blind sexual pollution of Oedipus; it has been re-enacted through history, by Dido, Cleopatra and Elizabeth I whose gorgeous trappings have not blinded the prophet to the essence of their acts. We are shown Lil and the typist stripped of any glamour to make us aware of the disturbing parallels which exist beyond appearance, beyond the 'gilded shell'. All the poem's lovers travesty in varying degrees the ideal erotic possibility shadowed forth in the Hyacinth garden which reminds the reader of the myth which none have achieved. Their deviation from this myth is further indicated by the way that each group is shown to have a kind of ritual. In the Hyacinth garden, the ritual of water and flowers is still close to the basic myth of generation, though tinged through the Hyacinth reference with the sacrifice of love; Madame Sosostris' ritual is payment and fussy caution; the Chess lovers, equally meaninglessly, have

> hot water at ten,
> And if it rains, a closed car at four.

To Lou, Lil and Albert it's the pub with its ritual closing time which becomes a reiteration of the threat of mortality: 'Hurry up please, it's time'. To the typist, it is food laid out in tins and bleak sexuality. To each group, there is a ritual pattern in living, but the patterns have lost all significance, becoming increasingly accidental.

If then the reader can accept a notion of simultaneous rather than developing order, each episode has to be experienced not in isolation as a single unit, but in conjunction with all the other episodes. The typist and clerk are part of *A Game of Chess*, of Lil and Albert and ultimately even of the Hyacinth garden pair. Such a notion is not merely a matter of intellectual scheme. Eliot is careful to plant echoes and parallels of detail to show the emotional relation between, for example, the house-agent's clumsy love-making and the higher failure of the quester before the maiden in the garden. He, under the pressure of deep emotion, cries

> I could not
> Speak, and my eyes failed, I was neither
> Living nor dead.

He retreats before a vision of ideal proffered love, while the young clerk, faced with the sordid actual, equally unresisting though indifferent, is also silent and manages only 'one bold stare'. He, too, having completed his assault, is blinded, not by 'the heart of light' but by 'finding the stairs unlit'. Neither, like Belladona who cries to her lover 'Do you see nothing', can see or know the significance of their experience. The irony of this parallel is clear. The clerk is as little like the Grail initiate of Romance tradition as it is possible to be, but when his way of life, which reduces the human potential to the automatic span of 'birth, copulation and death', is weighed against the lost vision of youth's quest for a life of natural and spiritual awareness, it is lifted from the plane of topical satire with music-hall overtones to that of permanent poetic comment. Compassion can be evoked at the same time as dismissive irony but the blend depends on seeing the scene in relation to other parallel encounters. The whole poem illustrates what Eliot described in a preface to Djuna Barnes *Nightwood* (1937) 'the deeper design . . . that of the human misery and bondage which is universal'. In terms of the poem's emotional range, it would be as distorting to single out this episode for Eliot's prevailing tone as it would be to offer the near ecstacy of the garden encounter. The total emotion of the poem covers the wide range between the two and is present in the all-inclusive consciousness which the episodes project, what Leavis in *New Bearings* (1932) described as 'the co-presence in the mind of a number of different orientations, fundamental attitudes, orders of expression'. The poem's tableaux are not self-sufficient, though separately framed. Their relation to each other is emotional. As I. A. Richards saw it in 1924:

> The items are united by the accord, contrast and interaction of their emotional effects. . . . The value lies in the unified responses which this interaction creates in the right reader.[11]

One of the aids to perceiving this unity in the poem is the way that its cast list of names, voices and pseudo-characters are held together by the shadow thrown by the Fisher King myths and the Tarot Pack of which Eliot admits in his notes having only a hazy knowledge—which leads him to make almost arbitrary connections between the two. One of the constant difficulties in interpretations of the poem is the tendency either to dismiss the importance of the legendary characters entirely, treating them as no more than casual points of reference, or to make categorical equations between these traditional figures and those of the poem. Even if we accept their importance in Eliot's own terms, as an ordering device, what is meant by claiming that Tiresias *is* the Fisher King, Madame Sosostris *is* the loathly hag or the Hyacinth girl *is* the Grail maiden? What kinds of identification are really intended, particularly in a poem, not a play, and one which has faces, voices and gestures rather than developing fictional characters?

The most obvious feature of *The Waste Land*'s cast-list is that it falls into even groups, two male and two female, two aged and two young. The Cumean Sibyl of the eipgraph sets the characteristic of the first female group, shrivelled away in body to a voice: old, burdened with a gift of prophecy and longing for death which she prophesies for others but cannot enjoy herself. Within her group come Madame Sosostris, *sage-femme*, and dear Mrs. Equitone, another reduced prophetess to whom life has lost all variety and distinction; Lil's friend with her 'sage' advice and Mrs. Porter, an old procuress. The younger women, some of them already past youth are all to a certain extent victims either

[11] I. A. Richards, 'The Poetry of T. S. Eliot', *Principles of Literary Criticism* (London, 2nd edn, 1926), appendix B, pp. 289–95.

of betrayed or failed love: Marie, whose one ecstatic memory was tinged with fear; Isolde who died for love; the Hyacinth girl who is already reminiscing—'You gave me hyacinths first a year ago'; Belladona, victim of her own nerves and of the hysterical relationship with her lover; Philomel, like the Sibyl reduced to an 'inviolable voice', but only through suffering at the hands of violent lust; Lil who looks 'so antique —(And her only thirty-one)', the typist in her semi-conscious indifference—

> Well now that's done: and I'm glad it's over.

and the Thames maiden who after the promise of 'a new start', 'made no comment'. The young men, merchant-travellers, soldiers and lovers are, in varying degrees, victims of the 'Death by water', Phlebas literally, others figuratively either in the sea as metaphor of passion or worldly preoccupation which dissolves mind and sensibility. There is the lover who fails before his vision of plenitude and becomes the 'I' who visits Madame Sosostris and moves through the 'Unreal City' to meet Stetson; then the lugubrious lover of Belladona who thinks 'we are in rat's alley', the demobbed Albert who 'wants a good time' as do 'the loitering heirs of city directors', Ferdinand and Sweeney who parodies the Grail ritual of washing of feet with Mrs. Porter and her daughter, Mr. Eugenides the dubious merchant, and the small house-agent's clerk, dismissed as 'one of the low', all of them involved in the ambivalent flame of lust and purgation which at the end of *The Fire Sermon* consumes and leads into the drowning of Phlebas. Phlebas is connected with the young erotic element of the group, being 'once handsome and tall as you', and with its commercial aspect through 'the profit and the loss'. The fourth group of aged male figures is the most elusive and fragmentary until it melts into the subsuming figure, Tiresias. They are either royal in status or prophetic in voice, first Marie's cousin the arch-duke, then Ezekiel who addresses the son of man in the desert (ll. 20–30), then the all-important 'I' found fishing in the dull canal in *The Fire Sermon*, who becomes a kind of link figure for the two male groups, being a Fisher King since he is

> Musing upon the king my brother's wreck

but also a Ferdinand, lover and quester figure, as he also muses

> on the king my father's death before him.

This dual identity, which incidentally establishes further the cyclical emphasis of the poem through generation, prepares the reader for the all-important Tiresias who, being both old and young, past and present, blind and seer, male and female incorporates in the final sections all four groups. He has both the role of observer in *The Fire Sermon* and *Death by Water* and participant as the representative ego who responds possibly to the three commands of the Thunder and emerges in the Fisher King guise

> sat upon the shore
> Fishing, with the arid plain behind me.

Perhaps the deliberate conflation of the Fisher King figure and the quester in Ferdinand was suggested by Jessie Weston's point that the sources differ about whether the wasting of the land is a cause of the king's sickness, wound or age, or is a result of the questing knight's own failure. She herself believes that the wasting of the land 'must be held to have been antecedent to that failure' but Eliot's syncretic intention in the poem seems deliberately to fuse the two causes making each curiously involved with the other. Thus the identification of Ferdinand, hearer of the transformation song—those are pearls that were his eyes—with the king himself is an important clue to the method of melting characters firstly into each other and finally into Tiresias, whose spectator's vision we are told in a note to line 218 is the poem's substance.

It is clear that the identification between the poem's 'cast' and the legendary figures and, even more so, the Tarot Pack, is fleeting and fragmentary rather than rigidly schematic. It operates with many shades of irony. The Grail maiden, for example, is traditionally supposed to chide the quester and probe into the causes of his failure at the Chapel. This perhaps lies behind the half resentful, half-plaintive tone of the Hyacinth girl's

> You gave me hyacinths first a year ago

and behind the very different nagging insistence of Belladona.

But beyond these occasional parallels, the overall link with the myth figures again bestows a shape, a form. This form is the consistent pattern of tensions between static King or prophet and dynamic quester, between static sage-femme and suffering maiden. It is in this, rather than in the projected speech of the pseudo-characters, that any truly dramatic quality in the poem lies. Critics have complained that the poem is too static and tableauesque. Vincent Buckley[12] analysed Eliot's whole poetic weakness in such terms, seeing him as a poet afraid to take account of 'this positive and dynamic quality in human life', a state in which 'emotions act' and are not merely conditions to be fixed and transmuted. Eliot's plays certainly show that the capture of speech idiom, though important, does not in itself constitute drama, and if *The Waste Land* is dramatic at all it is certainly not so in terms of emotional development. Rather, the dramatic pattern latent in the cycle of the myth, death—rebirth—death, is itself reflected in the participants, whose polarities of youth and age, action and suffering, provide an underlying pattern of tensions beneath the variety of episodes. These tensions form one of the many pairs of opposed symbols which run through the poem, illustrating the theme of death and rebirth; winter and spring, drought and rain, rock and water, silence and speech, seeing and blindness and action and frustration. The central symbolic action, fishing, though active, is only seen in the poem in its patient, unfulfilled condition. This, like the fusion of Ferdinand and the King, suggests a wish to blend the two states of action and suffering.

So, there is a series of layers of 'characters' in the poem. On its surface, sharply individuated in appearance, gesture and idiom are the multiple pseudo-figures (Marie, Lil and the rest) drawn apparently from observations of urban life and from the music hall. Immediately behind this layer, related to it by the comic figure of Madame Sosostris, present-day clairvoyant with her ridiculous Egyptian name, we have the figures and symbols from the Tarot Pack which she uses for commercial divination, hanged man, falling tower, last judgement, wheel. Miss Weston claims that these were used in divining the 'periodic rise and fall of the waters of the Nile' and the drying up of the Chinese flood waters. She also claims that the origin of the words used in the pack was Sanskrit or Hindustani, giving Eliot further substance for his attempt to fall back upon an Aryan bed-rock of tradition. In *The Burial of the Dead* Madame Sosostris introduces the poem's cast-list in terms of the Tarot figures, showing her own prophetic limitations in being unable to identify the one-eyed merchant's burden of mysteries or sins, and her inability to find the Hanged Man whether vegetation god-victim or sacrificed Son of God. Behind these is the third, most crucial layer, further reduced in number and having a synthesising function—the Grail legend figures, King, maiden and quester, to whom all the first layer personalities bear

[12] Vincent Buckley, *Poetry and Morality* (London, 1959), pp. 87–157.

some relation, metaphoric or ironic. The single, subsuming figure of Tiresias, serves, as does the Sanskrit in the poem, as a final unifying factor behind the fragmented races and languages, forming, as it were, the apex of a pyramid structure whose base is multiple but which is refined backwards in time to a single unity.

As a foresuffering seer and poet, Tiresias shows that the poem, for all its elaborations and its use of dramatic vignettes, is basically a lyrical observation on the present, confirmed by a metaphoric relation to past myths. These myths perform the function of projecting the poet's vision, for if the poet's ego is present at all, it is behind the ironic disguise of Tiresias who becomes a kind of 'objective correlative' or containing fiction for Eliot's own first voice. Being ancient and bi-sexual he can be credited with omniscience. Had the poet assumed this attribute *in propria persona* readers might well complain of emotions in excess of the facts.

If the mythological parallels help to establish a certain a-logical relation between the separate episodes of the poem, so does the basic emotional identity which lies behind scenic and idiomatic differentiation. This differentiation does strike the reader at first; there is a brilliant triumph in the way Eliot establishes contrasts of local atmosphere and place with the utmost economy of detail and suggestion. One of his persistent techniques is to switch atmospheres with almost crude speed:

> Looking into the heart of light, the silence.
> *Oed' und leer das Meer.*
>
> Madame Sosostris, famous clairvoyante,
> Had a bad cold. . . .

or more subtly:

> Pressing lidless eyes and waiting for a knock upon the door.
> When Lil's husband got demobbed I said

and most ironically daring, Parsifal's auditory vision of the adoration of the Grail:

> *Et, O ces voix d'enfants, chantant dans la coupole!*

modulating straight into the vulgar reduction of Philomel's inviolable voice:

> Twit twit twit,
> Jug jug jug jug jug jug

The perverse purpose of these shock contrasts is once more to jerk the reader into an awareness of the emotional identity beyond superficial differences. Though sharply and separately framed, the episodes share a basic group of predominant emotions, anxiety, fear, culminatin terror of mortality, ennui, purposelessness and a deep sense of thwarted climax maintained even in the ending.

It is Jessie L. Weston again who speculates that the initiation into life mysteries may well have involved encounter with death and the legends of the Chapel Perilous and the burial or drowning of the fertility god support this inevitable connection. To the inhabitants of Eliot's *Waste Land* these alternative extremes of life and death have become blurred; a theme startlingly summed up in the sardonic image of Stetson's 'sprouting corpse', in its context a parody of the corn effigy of nature rituals. Life in the waste takes on the colour and nature of a living death, hence the allusions to Dante's limbo state of 'neither living nor dead'. Hence too, the presence of the Sibyl and Tiresias who, though technically alive, are withered in the body and longing for death. Paradoxically, life seems to struggle out of death, 'lilacs out of the dead land', 'branches out of stony rubbish', Ferdinand's father out of supposed drowning. The link between the Sibyl and the Ezekiel line

> I will show you fear in a handful of dust

is crucial. The Sibyl has asked for as many years of life as she holds grains of sand and to the prophet, too, dust is symbol of mortality—'dust unto dust'. But in the waste land the fear of death, as to the Sibyl who forgot to ask for continued youth and vitality, has become a fear of life itself. Unlike her, the land's inhabitants are too afraid to want to die, but like her they are in a condition of unwanted life.

All are afraid; April inspires fear, Marie is frightened in her exultant moment, perhaps of sexual delight, on her cousin's sledge. The 'son of man' is exhorted to endure the vision of fear and mortality in the desert and the lover in the garden enters the limbo of the half-alive at the moment of initiation; Madame Sosostris actually counsels fear, of death by water; and the anxious crowd of Londoners, identified with the souls in Dante's Hell by the 'underground' image, exhale sighs. The much disputed dog, whether he stands for the Dog-days of hot desire, or for Humanitarianism, is to be feared as he will dig up what man hopes to hide, corpse or guilty memory. Trust has given way to fear. Belladona fears the torture of her own nerves, and fears too her lover, who is himself locked up in nightmare thoughts of mortality—'I think we are in rats' alley.' Lil fears Albert's return but fears equally (and is being destroyed by) the means she used to avert the fear of pregnancy.

In *The Fire Sermon*, fear and anxiety are replaced by the apathy, no less terrible, of the lonely woman stooping to folly with an indifferent lover, and of the Thames maidens whose fear has been lost in mental vacancy:

> On Margate sands.
> I can connect
> Nothing with nothing.

In *Death by Water* this anxious fear is given some relief in the actual drowning of Phlebas, but this too contains the warning of Mortality:

> Consider Phlebas, who was once handsome and tall as you.

In *What the Thunder said* terror is tempered by patience—

> We who were living are now dying with a little patience

but fear soon builds up again in the series of questions which challenge the reality of knowledge and experience—'who is the third' 'who is that' 'what is that sound' 'who are those hooded hordes' 'what is the city'? This fearful questioning reaches a climax in the nightmare hallucinations whether we take them naturalistically or as a version of the Chapel Perilous encounters.

The responses to the Thunder's commands are still fearful:

> blood shaking my heart
> The awful daring of a moment's surrender

> each in his prison
> Thinking of the key

and fear is one of the impulses behind the shoring up of fragments to ward off total ruin.

Such emotional identity helps the reader at first to orientate among the fragments of experience united by the poet in so subtle and oblique a way. Once these predominant emotions are established, the mind is free to respond to the intricate range of thematic links formed through tone and image. If logical means of linking are abandoned, they are replaced by an elaborate set of suggestive links which work through a process of echo and recall. An obvious example of this process can be examined in the relation between the woman in *A Game of Chess* and Lil in her cockney pub. The apparent contrast between the two is done in social terms, queen and pawn, conveyed in their different idioms:

'Speak to me. Why do you never speak. Speak', taut, neurotic but still preserving a certain polished control, and:

> It's them pills I took, to bring it off, she said

direct, robust, gossipy. But beneath such superficial difference of class both women are intrinsically the same, the society 'lady of situations' sick with ennui verging now on hysteria, Lil sunk in apathy. Both have sterile relationships in which all communication has broken down; both inhabit an erotic desert where perfumes are synthetic and natural functions are warped by bad nerves or chemist's pills. The lady who sits before her luxurious dressing-table amongst

> The glitter of her jewels

and

> Vials of ivory and coloured glass
> Unstoppered

is more alive in her trappings than in herself. The atmosphere is almost of an exotic tomb. She may indeed be ironically related to the corpse lying under a great golden candlestick which the Grail knight finds in the Chapel Perilous. The seven-branched candelabra incongruously recalls the Jewish 'Menorah' in this secular chamber and the 'staring forms, leaned out, leaning . . .' have something of the ghost quality associated with the Chapel. The attempted heightening of the jaded senses by artificial means culminating in their dissolution, 'drowned the sense in odours', is the experience craved by Sir Epicure Mamon in Jonson's *The Alchemist*. Lou, and poor Lil, toothless and worn out by child-birth has none of 'the arts that polish life'. Drably, she can only please Albert now with hot food, the 'gammon'. Yet the two women are one, and the unity between them is ironically established in minute details such as the word 'antique':

> You ought to be ashamed, I said, to look so antique.
> (And her only thirty-one.)

Behind this colloquialism, the word echoes the 'antique' of the 'antique mantel' in the lady's boudoir above which hangs the tapestry of Philomel, the legend of ravaged womanhood, which these two women are painfully reliving. It is to details of this kind, slight but vital, that the reader must grow alert.

Another and subtler example of this process of echo comes in the nightmare sequence of the falling towers and 'unreal' cities which shatter and crumble before the Thunder speaks. Many details of this nightmare recall those endured traditionally by the questers at the Chapel Perilous, in particular a curious half-light, the sounds of lamentation, the visions of death, a meeting with a woman and the finding of a belfry. The sudden close-up, reminiscent of a Hieronymus Bosch painting, which follows the fall of the distant cities contains such visions:

> A woman drew her long black hair out tight
> And fiddled whisper music on those strings
> And bats with baby faces in the violet light
> Whistled, and beat their wings
> And crawled head downward down a blackened wall
> And upside down in air were towers
> Tolling reminiscent bells

Carelessly read, this could seem merely a virtuoso piece of surrealistic nightmare, its ingredients drawn from private horrors or from war— evidence again of the author's preoccupation with the sordid. The almost Hopkinsian use of word-play to create the feel of decrescendo might be noted:

> crawled head downward down . . . and upside down

a verbal mimesis of falling. But the long black hair drawn out tight sends us back to the woman in *A Game of Chess*, her nerves now cracked into madness. There, her hair was 'spread out in fiery points', and there too it made as if to speak

> Glowed into words, then would be savagely still.

This savagery is now fulfilled in mad music. Then, she had neurotically threatened to rush out into the street 'with my hair down, so', hair dry and fiery with the frustration of love, sharply contrasted with the life-promising Hyacinth girl:

> Your arms full, and your hair wet.

And somewhere between the two, indifferent, neither dry nor lush and wet, is the hair of the typist who, looking momentarily into a glass, just as Belladona gazed into hers:

> smoothes her hair with automatic hand

It is no fanciful accident that the mad music is played upon female hair, the sustained image offering the theme of thwarted or perverted love which all these women exemplify. Only bats have 'baby' faces in the whole poem, there is no 'laughter of children among leaves', and the bats' 'upsidedownness' reminds us of Lil's despairing perversion of birth through abortion. Moreover, the upside-down vision of falling towers— even the Grail belfry is inverted like a reflection in water—takes us back to the curious reflections and shifts of visual perspective in the lady's boudoir.

> Doubled the flames of sevenbranched candelabra
> Reflecting light upon the table as
> The glitter of her jewels rose to meet it

Everything in the boudoir is an example of man-made luxury, ornate to a point of decadence. Every material has been shaped by man; burnished marble, coloured glass, wrought metal, jewels, carved stone, painting and tapestry. She is decked with all the arts, but the hint of evil comes in the way art is here rivalling, distorting, not merely enhancing Nature. For such a favourite Renaissance theme Eliot adopts a Spenserian technique to emphasise the lady's removal from the natural sphere. Her glass is

> Held up by standards wrought with fruited vines

and has one cupid boy peeping out suggestively, another hiding his eyes flirtatiously behind his wing. The eye is deliciously cheated with double reflections; we are not far from Acrazia's Bower of Bliss. The satin cases, vials of ivory, synthetic perfumes—a morally loaded word—the coffered ceiling and carved mantel and the tapestry, itself imitating a window opening on to a 'silvan scene', constitute a pseudo-paradise. This is achieved by an almost Baroque 'trompe-l'œil' effect. But it is a claustro-phobic paradise, the real fresh air which enters is soon mingled and dissipated by the candle smoke. The result on man is synaesthesia, the sensual confusion wrought not only by the mixture of odours but by the breakdown of the outlines of the senses and even of the basic elements. On a literal level the 'geography' of the room may be quite clear; a patterned, coffered ceiling, a fire burning in the antique stone grate with a tapestry of Philomel above it. But by the echoing play of images, the senses dissolve into each other, drowning personal identity, and the very elements and their associated colours, fire and water, orange and green, merge into each other confusedly. The burning wood is from the sea and is now consumed by fire and so burns green as well as orange. The wood, being 'sea-wood fed with copper', is confused by sound—association with the coffered wood of the ceiling on which the reflection of fire and candlelight is thrown, wood becoming first fire, then light.

The dolphin swims not in water but in 'sad light'. As this lady is recalled in the lady who fiddles, Nero–like, on her hair among falling towers, so the confused blending of senses and elements into a synaesthetic 'drowning' is only one step away from the kinaesthetic nightmare of the later upside–down sequence. There, confusion has lost all aesthetic pleasure and is frenzied, accompanied by the whisper music of the mad woman and the parched voices

> singing out ot empty cisterns and exhausted wells.

It is through recurrent images, such as the hair which links these episodes, that Eliot establishes the emotional and thematic unity of his apparently diverse fragments. It is also noticeable that these images seem to fall into patterned groups; for example, an underlying pattern of the four elements is discernible in *The Waste Land*, though in a far less schematic form than in the later *Four Quartets*.* From earth comes the group of images of aridity, stunted growth and mortal decay, 'dull roots', 'dried tubers', 'stony rubbish', 'dead trees', 'dust', 'dry stone', 'bones', 'rattled by the rats foot', 'currants' (being shrivelled grapes), 'wrinkled dugs', 'trams and dusty streets', 'Margate Sands', 'the broken fingernails of dirty hands', all culminating in the extreme dryness of the desert in V where

> Sweat is dry and feet are in the sand

and we look into the

> Dead mountain mouth of carious teeth that cannot spit . . .

We hear 'dry sterile thunder' and meet people peering 'from doors of mudcracked houses', travel along a sandy road with 'dry singing grass' and desiccated trees that wait with 'limp leaves' meeting hordes 'stumbling in cracked earth' among 'empty cisterns' and 'exhausted wells'.

Complementing these strongly physical images is the pattern of the desiccated human encounters and relationships where both pains and pleasures are reduced and withered in the limbo condition and the locked tower of selfhood prevents communication.

* For a very interesting account of Eliot's possible debt to Colin Still, *Shakespeare's Mystery Play: A Study of the Tempest* (London, 1921) see Ronald Tamplin, 'The Tempest and The Waste Land', *American Literature* (1967), pp. 352–72.

Mr. Tamplin, arguing that Still's book is 'the intermediate and decisive source' between Weston and Frazer and *The Waste Land*, offers an ingenious reading of the poem in which the four elements are seen to correspond to the 'passional' and 'celestial' spheres of the lower and higher paradises of spiritual initiation.

Linked with earth through the desert winds is the second element, air. There is first the 'fresh' wind which was to blow Isolde to land and which is clearly related to the air that 'freshened from the window' in Belladona's claustrophobic boudoir. Neither wind resists pollution by the atmosphere it plays upon, the love potion and the unstoppered vials. Belladona is frightened by the noise of 'the wind under the door'. In *The Fire Sermon* the same wind crosses the brown land but is silent, 'unheard', until it becomes the 'cold blast' of the terrified sense of mortality 'at my back'. A 'brisk swell', a south-west wind, carried Elizabeth and Leicester's 'gilded shell' down the Thames and gets up again for its climax in the empty chapel, called 'only the wind's home'. The door swings and cockcrow at last releases lightning and the damp gust. The fresh wind reappears, implicitly at least, in the third command where the sea was calm and propitious for a surrender of the heart, gaily, 'to controlling hands'. But *would have* shows that, like the Hyacinth garden surrender, this remains a 'might have been'.

Much more complex than earth and air are the other antithetical pair, fire and water. Eliot draws upon every kind of association in these two elements, often deliberately confusing the two where both can symbolise the same idea.

From Dante and from Christian and Buddhist ascetic tradition, Eliot takes over the paradoxical symbol of fire as both the flame of lust and sensual attachment (and the consequent fire of vengeful destruction), and yet as the purifying flame of purgation. Hence *The Fire Sermon*, with its climactic fusion of St. Augustine's 'cauldron of unholy loves' and Buddha's sermon in:

> Burning burning burning burning
> O Lord Thou pluckest me out . . .

The purgatorial aspect of fire is earlier established in the sun that beats upon the 'son of man' in the desert passage. The 'red rock' in whose shadow he is invited to shelter has been variously interpreted as the rock of the God of Israel, the rock in the traditional landscapes of the Grail knight's testing, as the red-granite rocks of Eliot's childhood in Missouri landscape and as the red mountain of Dante's *Purgatorio*; it may well be an amalgam of all these, but at the most immediate level of sensual apprehension it seems hot and fiery, a shelter in extremity, but not a cool retreat. Fire surrounds the sensual but sterile lady of situations. She sits on a burnished throne beneath the flames of a seven-branched candelabra. There is a huge sea-wood fire whose green and orange light is described as sad rather than warm, and her hair, 'spread out in fiery points', like the flames surrounding the souls in Dante's *Purgatorio* which glow as they speak, glows savagely rather than brilliantly. The 'Beauty' of Lil and Albert's life is reduced to the heat of hot gammon and the 'sun's last rays' usual romantic associations are punctured in their context, where they touch, not the typist's skin, but 'her drying combinations'. The treasure of the Rhine maidens, their golden cups sometimes interpreted as the elements of warmth and sunlight reflected in the depths of water, are stolen with their chastity. *What the Thunder Said* opens with 'torchlight red on sweaty faces' and intense, vibrant heat is engendered by suggestion in the trudge through the desert, surely a purgatorial journey. The sun is setting, the air violet, but the heat goes on until the flash of lightning which releases the wind 'over Himavant' and the hot 'jungle crouched'. Finally, it is the purgatorial aspect of fire which is stressed in the desperate fragments through the allusion to Dante's *Purgatorio* (XXVI, 148), where Arnaut Daniel willingly leaps back into the flames which represent the lusts of his life. 'Poi s'ascose nel foco che gli affina', 'affina' containing the only hope he still has to be 'redeemed from fire by fire'.

Thus fire combines with earth to cause the dust, red rock and the nightmarish red faces and is a convenient traditional symbol for passionless human desires which burn dryly, destructively.

Water is even more complex as a sustaining symbol, being the principal symbol in Jessie L. Weston's life cults as 'the freeing of the waters'. Eliot retains this aspect of water symbolism only fleetingly in his poem. Nearly always it is over-shadowed by the threat of the waste land itself. Thus 'spring rain' is part of April's cruelty, and the summer shower drives Marie and her cousin to shelter and is provided against by Belladona and her lover in their closed car. Yet when it is absent, it is strongly desired. It is lamented that amongst the dry stone there is 'no sound of water', and later in the last desert extremity the marvellously conjured aural mirage of water intensifies this craving:

> If there were rock
> And also water
> And water
> A spring
> A pool among the rock
> If there were the sound of water only . . .
> Drip drop drip drop drop drop drop . . .

The reader is caught up in the parched longing which, through the association of rock and water, alluding to Moses' smiting of the rock in the desert to bring forth waters of salvation, is of spiritual as well as physical significance. The poem's moments of nearly missed ecstasy are associated with moisture. Marie in the mountain snows, the Hyacinth girl with her wet hair and the very succulent lushness of her flowers contributing as much to their sexual symbolism as the allusion to the Hyacinth myth. But against this group of lush associations of water are set the powerful group of drowning, rotting, and corrosive aspects of water. This ambivalence begins in the Wagnerian allusions. In *Tristan and Isolde*, the sea which should bring Isolde to Tristan is described as 'Oed' und leer', waste and void, signifying the hungry desolation bred by the surrender to the love potion by the two at sea, a craving which can only be assuaged by death. Madame Sosostris, finding the drowned sailor in her pack of cards, begins the whole train of drowning images: these being as paradoxical as flames, since drowning is fearful, involving the loss of bodily life—'Consider Phlebas, who was once handsome and tall as you'—but can also be a means of purification, cleansing and transforming, 'those are pearls that were his eyes' being spoken of a corpse supposedly drowned. This transformation aspect is repeated in the Ariel song several times, by Madame Sosostris, without understanding; it is afloat in the mind of Belladona's lugubrious lover, though he reduces the allusion to 'that Shakespeherean rag'.† The terrifying aspect is recalled in *Death by Water* where Phlebas' bones are picked 'in whispers'. Ironically, the dwellers in the land, consultants of Madame Sosostris, are only aware of the bodily terror, hence 'fear death by water' and the 'current under sea', the whirlpool which separates man for ever from his body and from 'the profit and the loss' so important to his material existence. For Eliot also uses the sea traditionally as the sea of life on which man is a bark afloat, hence the image of the wheel, on the one hand the steering wheel by which man controls his existence—'O you who turn the wheel' and the crucial image of 'the hand expert with sail and oar'—but on the other, the arbitrary wheel of fortune which spins men's destinies. One of the poem's narrowly missed opportunities is related to the wheel in the response to the third command which speaks of a heart which *would have* responded gaily,

when invited, beating obedient
To controlling hands.

But it is 'would have'; instead the heart becomes one of the crowd, walking in an aimless circle:

> I see crowds of people, walking round in a ring.

This same crowd metaphorically 'flows' over London Bridge in the 'unreal city', further suggesting the ambivalence of the water imagery, their flow being not vital but shapeless as the swarming of the 'hooded hordes'. Nor is there any union between the individuals in the crowd. They do not flow together but retain their isolation as 'each man fixed his eyes before his feet', locked in selfhood.

The poem's men of the sea are similarly two-sided. There is the grotesque Stetson, 'you who were with me in the ships at Mylae', a sailor but linked to the world of profit and loss by fighting in the commercial Punic Wars and again in the 1914–18 war. The one-eyed merchant has come from the sea bringing not mysterious life cults, but currants for trade C.i.f. Phlebas was part of this world before his immersion in the 'deep sea swell'.

Against this are set Ferdinand and his father, rescued magically from the sea, from false grief and from sin, hearing the song of transformation:

> This music crept by me upon the waters.

There is the faintly glimpsed society of fishmen associated with the 'pleasant whining of a mandoline' near the wall of Magnus Martyr, the church connected through its patron saint with escape from persecution by leaping into the sea. This aspect of water is the strongest link with the Fisher King myth via the fish, symbol of teeming fertility and by association, mysterious wisdom. There is a further complication in the fact that fresh river waters, in *The Waste Land*, have either dried up or suffered pollution by man so that the poem's rivers become an aspect of the waste itself. Even the full river at the beginning of *The Fire Sermon* is presented in forbidding terms, suggestive of rape and drowning rather than of elemental vitality:

> the last fingers of leaf
> Clutch and sink into the wet bank.

The Thames of Spenser's *Prothalamion* did not bear the 'empty bottles, sandwich papers, silk handkerchiefs, cardboard boxes, cigarette ends' which litter the modern river, partly because it was evoked in a context of marriage ceremony celebrated by rituals of promised fertility. Now the river is polluted with 'testimony of summer nights' of casual love and dalliance present too in the 'waters of Leman', which puns characteristically on the Swiss lake name and the medieval word for paramour. The river banks are correspondingly rotten, a place for a rat to drag its slimy belly. Fishers seek even the dull canal rather than the river as source of lively fish. Feet are washed not in holy water but in soda water, and the river 'sweats' as Eliot describes it in terms reminiscent of Conrad's Thames in the opening of *Heart of Darkness*, another work where a river becomes a symbol for the penetration of corruption, not vitality. When we reach the Ganga (Ganges) before the Thunder breaks, it is sunken.

It is from this complex use of water-symbolism that the reader may derive a tentative sense of the significance of the total Waste Land experience. For the emotional weight in the poem seems to suggest that salvation from waste for man must lie more in the direction of the ambivalent sea than of rain or river water. There is need for a transformation, not merely for the restoration of a lost natural flow. Jungian interpretation of the poem can go too far when applied in too detailed a way, but in general what Jung described as 'the collapse of the conscious attitude [which] at first feels like the end of the world' may well lie behind the use of the sea in the poem as a symbol of man's own subconscious mind into which he must make a terrifying descent, surrendering the wheel of control by personal will, to the unknown power of the sea, control from without.† Through this elemental surrender man can perhaps achieve transformation as he might through surrender to purgatorial flames. The mortality, the picking of his bones, will be perhaps the price for the sea-change 'into something rich and strange'.

In the fertility myths of *The Golden Bough* Frazer tells how the god's image was sometimes buried and sometimes cast into the sea to be washed up and 're-born' before the celebration of new life. The burial aspect of these myths is sardonically dismissed in the Stetson encounter:

> That corpse you planted last year in your garden,
> Has it begun to sprout? Will it bloom this year?

The tone is anything but reverential, the allusion to the myth and to 'the dead shall be raised incorruptible' of the Pauline Burial service entirely ironic. But it may be that when Tiresias emerges at the end, it is significant that he is fishing 'upon the shore', therefore in the sea, the agent of change, rather than in the river. Perhaps the river is a lost source of natural vitality and no longer the right medium for the quester's search. As the spring stirring of life inspired fear, so perhaps the terrors of drowning are to be endured despite fear. Like the near ecstasy in the Hyacinth Garden, the missed moment recorded in the response to the third command has the tone almost of a lovers' invitation to a dance:

> your heart would have responded
> Gaily, when invited, beating obedient
> To controlling hands. . .

It is again a 'might have been' but in the poem's form of cyclic progression, it remains to the reader's imagination perhaps a 'perpetual possibility'.

2. *The Web of Allusion*

Hieronymo: As you, my Lord, in Latin, I in Greek,
                 You in Italian, and for because I know
                 That Bellimperia hath practised the French
                 In courtly French shall all her phrases be.
Balthasar: But this will be a mere confusion,
                 And hardly shall we all be understood.
Hieronymo: It must be so! for the conclusion
                 Shall prove the invention and all was good.
Thomas Kyd, *The Spanish Tragedy* Act IV, sc. I, II, 174–82.

To turn the capacity of recognising recondite references into a shibboleth by which culture may be estimated is a perversion to which scholarly persons are too much addicted.
    I. A. Richards, *Principles of Literary Criticism* (London, 1924), p. 218

I

One of the main issues to disturb the early reviewers of *The Waste Land* was of course the extraordinary amount of patent and disguised literary allusion in Eliot's text. Adverse critics were quick to conclude from Eliot's allusive technique that he was not a 'true poet' looking directly upon life and drawing poetic material from it, but a pseudo-poet who looks at it and draws from it only through the spectacles of books, and books in seven languages at that. Many had the 'democratic' fear that such poetry would be directed at an increasingly small audience of supersophisticated literary scholars. Historically, these critics could dismiss Eliot's way of writing too summarily as a clever reaction to effete Georgian poetry and 'poetics'. A typical view was that of Richard Aldington (while he was still a co-editor of *The Criterion* with Eliot):

> the poetry of T. S. Eliot is a healthy reaction against the merely pretty and agreeable, against shallowness and against that affectation of simplicity which verged on dotage.[13]

But many readers then, and many now, feel that Eliot's avoidance of sweet simplicity led him to a method of writing so erudite as to be chilling and 'anti-life'. Even sensitive critics like Conrad Aiken[14] complained that 'in *The Waste Land* Mr. Eliot's sense of the literary past has almost become the motive of the work.' It is 'a poetry not more actuated by life itself than by poetry.' Literature was perhaps becoming a sort of mistletoe on literature. Eliot himself would probably have answered any philistine distinction between literature and life with the assertion made in an introduction to Ezra Pound's highly allusive verse: 'The ordinary life of ordinary cultivated people is a mush of literature and life.'[15] The experience of a sunset, for example, in a painting or poem, may be even more memorable than an actual sunset precisely because of the more active participation of the mind in the absence of direct sense stimuli. We expect art to sharpen and extend our awareness of the significance of experience. Thus, to allude to Marvell's *To his Coy Mistress* is to allude not to an arid anthology piece, but to a moving analysis of erotic desire in the context of fear of mortality which may constitute acute experience for its readers.

But many early readers of *The Waste Land* felt with F. L. Lucas[16] that Eliot 'replaces depth by muddiness, beauty by echoes, passion by necrophily'. The poem is 'ill-knit, loaded with echo and allusion, fantastic and crude, obscure and obscurantist'. Less angrily, Clive Bell[17] complained:

> He cannot write in the great manner out of the heart of his subject; his verse cannot gush as a stream from the rock; bird-like he must pile up wisps and straws of recollection round the tenuous twig of a central idea.

[13] R. Aldington, 'The Poetry of T. S. Eliot', essay in *Literary Studies and Reviews* (London, 1924), pp. 181–91.

[14] C. Aiken, review in *The New Republic* (Feb. 7th, 1923), reprinted in *T. S. Eliot, The Man and his Work*, ed. Allen Tate (London, 1967), pp. 194–203.

[15] T. S. Eliot, preface to *Selected Poems of Ezra Pound* (London, 1928), p. xi.

[16] F. L. Lucas, review in *The New Statesman* (Nov. 3rd, 1923), pp. 116–18.

[17] Clive Bell, review in *Nation and Atheneum* (Sept. 22nd 1923), pp. 772–3.

What these early reviewers seemed to miss was the immediate emotional power and authority of tone of the poem. Lucas would have scorned the view that this force, expressing, as it does, a central idea which few would seriously relegate to a 'tenuous twig', can communicate before the whole text is understood, though Eliot himself held this position. Their suspicion sprang from what T. E. Hulme in the posthumous *Speculations* called a critical attitude of mind which demands romantic qualities of verse although the Romantic tradition itself was running dry in the annual Georgian output. With hindsight, we are in a better position to detect an essentially Romantic tone underneath the poem's ironic surface.

Sympathetic reviews anticipated more closely reservations which, even today, although we are being educated to recognise the allusive elements in Medieval, Augustan and even Romantic poetry, we may retain about the allusive technique peculiar to this poem. It is significant that after *The Waste Land*, Eliot continued to allude, but in a more general way, rationing the element of fragmentary verbal snatchings. Some did see in his earlier technique, culminating in *The Waste Land*, hints of a thwarted or frightened Romantic, needing to hide a pained sensibility behind 'Laforgian' ironic masks, or assumed personae; Prufrock, the agèd eagle (when still in his early 30's), Gerontion and Tiresias, the embodiment perhaps of his contemporary theory of an 'objective correlative', if we understand by this much-abused phrase, a containing fiction for the poet's ideas and feelings. The note that 'what Tiresias *sees*, in fact, is the substance of the poem' suggests not so much that he is the technical 'I' or protagonist throughout, but that he is the mythological figure, chosen to stand for and contain the whole of human experience. Being both male and female, having prophetic vision and having lived through immense age, spanning history, he is the poem's containing fiction, being beyond the accidents of place, time and personality. But this figure is at most an objectifying mask for the poet's own personality and voice. Aiken himself found everywhere in the poem 'evidence of a delicate personality, somewhat shrinking, somewhat injured and always sharply itself'.

The general objections to Eliot's allusive method could be answered by shoring up quotations from his own criticism against private critical misgivings. We know from *Tradition and the Individual Talent* that he was attempting to write a poem with not merely his own generation in his bones, but with a feeling that the whole of the literature of his own country and of Europe had a simultaneous existence. At one level, the poem's allusions can be seen as a way of bringing the whole of literature to bear upon the situation described, giving it historical and geographical dimension. We may remember too in the essay on Massinger, 1926: 'Immature poets imitate, mature poets steal' and, less aphoristically, his claim that

> the good poet welds his theft into a whole of feeling which is unique, utterly different from that from which it was torn.

While Eliot believed that originality of material could only lead to eccentricity, true originality lay for him in 'an original way of assembling the most disparate material to form a new whole' (*The Frontiers of Criticism*, 1956).

It is futile to debate the essential validity of an allusive technique. For some it will always be a vulgarly ostentatious display of pseudo-learning, for others a true way of gaining density in a compressed text. Ultimately this becomes a matter of personal taste and literary fashion rather than of argument. But it is clearly important to determine Eliot's success or failure in welding his thefts into a whole of feeling. Certainly *The Waste Land*, its essence and tone, cannot be traced to any one of its sources; but Conrad Aiken in 1923 and Graham Hough[18] in a serious attack in 1960 both disputed Eliot's success in achieving a new 'whole of feeling'. Aiken felt he

> had not wholly annealed the allusive matter, has left it unabsorbed, lodged its gleaming fragments amid material alien to it,

and Hough complained that the poem mixed its modes too drastically and so lacked the essential unity of 'one voice speaking'. Such a distinctive and cohesive voice is all-important in a poem so full of masks and imitated voices, and lacking the unity usually provided by narrative or discursive threads. Perhaps because the poem is so condensed we are less prepared for a range of mode and voice from mock-heroic:

> the evening hour that strives
> Homeward, and brings the sailor home from sea,
> The typist home at teatime, clears her breakfast

to the highly charged lyricism of

> Your arms full, and your hair wet, I could not
> Speak, and my eyes failed

though we might accept and even demand such variety from an epic of conventional length. To Hough, the parts are assembled but not

[18] G. Hough, *Image and Experience* (London, 1960), pp. 3–83.

welded. The only answer to such criticism is that the residue, when all the source hunters have done their work, is precisely a governing voice, tone and emotion which comes through the surface variety, allusive though this be.

Eliot was himself aware of the need for wholeness of feeling, for a poem which is more than the sum of its traceable parts. *The Waste Land* was written at a period when he was interested in the theory of the poet as inheritor and bearer of tradition. In alluding to a body of literature which he may hope (perhaps fondly in the case of some of his allusions) will be the common heritage of poet and audience, the poet will at least be able to prevent his allusions from becoming too private, too confined to personality. In *The Use of Poetry and the Use of Criticism* Eliot did admit that there were moments, or memories which have unconscious meaning and importance for the poet, amounting almost to a private symbolism:

> The song of one bird, the leap of one fish, at a particular place and time, the scent of one flower, an old woman on a German mountain path, six ruffians playing cards at nightfall at a small French railway junction where there was a water-mill. Such memories have a symbolic value, but of what we cannot tell, for they come to represent the depths of feeling into which we cannot peer.

Here, his insistence on the private and subrational quality of allusions to rare experience suggests that Eliot would make no qualitative distinction between these allusions and those to phrases, scenes or whole works of literature which bear for him a similar symbolic value. One has only to remember how much he attached to the touch-stone line from Dante 'In his will is our peace' to realise the parallel. The poem was concerned with the public communication of his theories of tradition and history and with bringing the past to bear upon the present by juxtaposing fragments from many periods in one text. Hence the suggestion, audacious for 1917, that

> We shall often find that not only the best, but the most individual parts of a poet's work may be those in which the dead poets, his ancestors, assert their immortality most vigorously.

But this theoretical position leaves many questions unanswered. Since Eliot could maintain that tradition is a living body which is changed and modified each time it is added to by new works, does not this imply, for example, that Marvell's *To his Coy Mistress* is not the same poem, now that it has its ironic fragmentary place in Eliot's twentieth-century poem?

Is it through being quoted and alluded to in borrowed and stolen phrases, rhythms and total atmospheres that 'the dead poets, his ancestors, assert their immortality', or is it, much less specifically, that they assert themselves in general as formative influences on the developing poet and his style? (See: *To Criticize the Critic*, 1965). What is certain is that Eliot saw his allusive technique as part of the inevitable complexity of modern art:

> The poet must become more and more complex, more allusive, more indirect, in order to force, to dislocate if necessary, language into its meaning.
>
> *Metaphysical Poets*, 1921

I. A. Richards[19] had prophesied similarly in 1924 that poets would become more and more allusive and specialised because

> Allusion is the most striking of the ways in which poetry takes into its service elements and forms of experience which are not inevitable to life but need to be specially acquired.

Aware perhaps of the dangers of exclusiveness in this plea for a stiffening of the intellectual status of poetry, Richards also warned:

> Allusion is a trap for the writer almost as effective as for the academic critic. It invites insincerity; it may encourage and disguise laziness, when it becomes a habit it is a disease.

If the habit becomes too automatic, evading proper poetic definition for the poet and literary analysis for the critic, it defeats its own end and poetry degenerates into a cross-word puzzle to be solved intellectually. *The Waste Land* is too often treated in this way; one might cite the annual debt to Eliot of the columns of *Notes and Queries*.

Eliot made his own position on the source-hunting critical approach clear. Discussing Livingston Lowes' *The Road to Xanadu* in *The Frontiers of Criticism*, 1956, he praises it but declares

> No one, after reading the book, could suppose that he understood *The Ancient Mariner* any better; nor was it in the least Dr. Lowes' intention to make the *poem* more intelligible as poetry. He was engaged on an investigation of process . . . the book is a fascinating bit of detection.

[19] I. A. Richards, *Principles of Literary Criticism* (London, 2nd edn. 1926), pp. 215–18.

D

The same attitude is evident in Eliot's famous dismissal of the importance of his own Notes to *The Waste Land*. Conceived 'in order to provide a few more pages of printed matter' they were regretted by Eliot precisely because they had stimulated the wrong kind of critical approach, the goose-chase after definitive sources, if not after the Grail itself.

However we may agree with Eliot that the notes are 'bogus scholarship'—and certainly they are provokingly incomplete and sometimes clearly facetious in tone (see note to l. 357)—they were never withdrawn, and it is clearly impossible to ignore the leads they give or to deny the powers of recognition of one's own mind or that of more widely read commentators. There is an essential difference between what Eliot called 'process' in, say, *The Ancient Mariner*, which also draws upon multiple and esoteric sources, and *The Waste Land*. The assimilation of the source material is different in kind and results in a difference of surface texture which makes the reader's problems quite different in the two cases. Where *The Waste Land* beckons the reader by the bristling echoes and fragments which make up its outer texture, it is quite possible to read stanzas of *The Ancient Mariner* without being aware of Coleridge's reading at all. Lowes can reveal that almost every phrase in lines like

> But where the ship's huge shadow lay,
> The charmèd water burned alway
> A still and awful red

(ll. 269-71)

is 'caught from the pages of Mortens and Cook', authentic sea-voyagers, and 'charmèd water' may well have come from Milton's 'charmèd wave' To be aware of this is to be given a tool towards analysing the processes of Coleridge's verbal and visual assimilation, but it is not necessary to our response to the text, nor does it solve the kind of problems of meaning and symbols which the poem poses. Some of Eliot's sources too seem to be of this kind. For example, his debt to Conrad's *Heart of Darkness* for his evocation of the Thames estuary (ll. 266-77) or to Joyce's *Ulysses*, in particular to Paddy Dingnam's funeral in the Hades episode, for some of the rats' alley and gashouse and canal imagery, is interesting but by no means essential to our response and understanding. Phrases will naturally catch the ear of a poet with this kind of 'auditory imagination' as musical phrases will a composer. In neither Eliot's nor Coleridge's case does the recognition of source or allusion explain the meaning or define the tone of the poem, but the difference is that whereas with Coleridge their discovery and investigation seem optional, in Eliot's poem they often seem inevitable. We cannot pass over a whole stanza in German which we may or may not recognise, nor can we ignore the familiar sonority of

> Son of Man . . .
> . . . I will show you fear in a handful of dust.

Even in translation, the idiom of a line like

> I had not thought death had undone so many,

with its slightly archaic use of tense, is bound to arrest us in a poem which is also to contain the cockney idiom of

> What you get married for if you don't want children?

When we reach

> The Chair she sat in, like a burnished throne,
> Glowed on the marble,

recognition is followed by a sense that it is not quite right, until we realise that here Eliot is echoing the rhythmic and metrical casing exactly, only subtly changing the words so that we immediately wonder why.

Once we begin to answer that question we come upon one of the greatest dangers in reading *The Waste Land*, that of resting in a delighted sense of discovered *meaning* because we have recognised an allusion. Eliot himself warned about the heresy of 'meaning'.

> The chief use of the 'meaning' of a poem, in the ordinary sense, may be . . . to satisfy one habit of the reader, to keep his mind diverted and quiet, while the poem does its work upon him.

Here again Eliot comes close to a Romantic doctrine, the desire to quiet that part of the mind which shows an 'irritable reaching after fact and reason . . . being incapable of remaining content with half knowledge'. But the allusions in the poem are not just a sop to the 'irritable' intellect. Some are of superficial importance, phrases used because they have struck the poet's ear and imagination. Others belong to the poem's substance and are part of what works upon us.

If, as some feared, the allusions remain as 'gleaming fragments' they may have an intellectual and emotional value of their own for the reader, coming from their original contexts and not necessarily relevant to Eliot's new 'whole of feeling'. Conversely, they may have a private symbolic value for Eliot which is hidden to us. If, after preliminary recognition, the reader tries to make equations, very often the two sides do not seem to fit. Seeming parallels turn out to be ironic contrasts and hidden parallels emerge from differences. Knowledge of the original context may even blur Eliot's intended effect and make us insensitive to the new tone and context. Thus the first and most crucial problem for the reader to decide is how much and in what tone the original context is being transported by implication into the poem. As Northrop Frye[20] warns, we cannot assume 'that the emotional effect of the original can simply be added to Eliot's poem'.

II

There are areas of the poem where the text is so dense with echoes and references that it amounts almost to a patchwork or to something like imitation, in the eighteenth-century sense. Eliot believed in practice by imitation. In *The Music of Poetry*, 1942, he declared:

> The only way to learn to manipulate any kind of English verse seemed to be by assimilation and imitation, by becoming so engrossed in the work of a particular poet that one could produce a recognisable derivative.

Now that the drafts are available they confirm Eliot's memory of what Pound had excised from his poem. It did originally contain a piece of direct stylistic imitation. He said:

> It contained some stanzas in imitation of Pope, and Ezra said to me 'Pope's done that so well that you'd better not try to compete with him', which was sound advice.

Although the edited text has no passages of direct imitation of any single sustained style, there are moments when the allusive method amounts to a kind of multiple imitation. Of these, the most striking and sustained is the 'set-piece' description of Belladona. It is possible to provide a literary source for almost every phrase and detail of this portrait ranging from Plutarch to Pater.[21] The method of suggesting

[20] Northrop Frye, *T. S. Eliot* (Edinburgh, 1963), p. 27.
[21] Giorgio Melchiori, *The Tight-rope Walkers* (London, 1956), pp. 53–88.

moral qualities by outward trappings is done very
manner. Eliot is creating an emblematic figure,
who is at the same time a syren queen, temptress
and a suffering victim in love herself, lonely and l

> My nerves are bad tonight. Yes, bad. Sta

Behind the verbal echoes out of which the portra
traditional figures, the whore of Babylon and Philomel. Both these are
found elsewhere in the poem, but they centre here. Belladona is, after
all, the whore of Eliot's 'unreal city', the bedecked woman of luxury.
The link with Babylon is suggested later in the punning reference to
'the waters of Leman' which twists the familiar psalmist's 'waters of
Babylon' where the Israelites wept in exile, to Leman, the lake where
Eliot in convalescence composed part of his poem. The Great Whore in
the bible is 'arrayed in purple and scarlet colour and decked with gold
and precious stones' and 'sitteth upon many waters', as did Cleopatra in
her barge on Cydnus in Shakespeare's play and in his source in Plutarch's
Lives. The tapestry on the wall, showing the change of Philomel from
woman to bird after her violation by Tereus, gives the other fundamental
side of the portrait. It looks forward to the allusions to other women
victims of betrayed or brutalised love, to Ophelia, through the 'good-
night, sweet ladies' (l. 172) and to the 'undone' Thames maiden who
can connect 'nothing with nothing' on Margate sands, the other place
incidentally where Eliot was convalescing during the composition of his
poem.

Between these two background figures who again form the apex of a
receding triangle whose base is the surface text, are ranked many legendary and literary women. What I have called the Renaissance quality
of the portrait lies in the way in which the character and significance of
the figure are to be deduced from the objects which surround and even
swamp her. Her association with historical and literary predecessors is an
essential part of this aura. Of Belladona herself, we are only given
gestures; she is gazing into a mirror, presumably brushing her hair.

Enobarbus' formal encomium on Cleopatra, itself derived from
Plutarch's set piece, is clearly in Eliot's mind, hence his 'theft' with
significant alteration of the exact metrical pattern of its first lines:

> The Chair she sat in, like a burnished throne,
> Glowed on the marble,

* For a discussion of the tradition of the Sibyl lying behind the dual
aspect of womanhood, see G. Grover Smith, 'T. S. Eliot's Lady of the
Rocks', *Notes and Queries*, CXCIV (1949), pp. 123–5.

...ery changes, *barge* to *chair*, *burned* to *glowed* and *water* to *marble*, ...emphasise the static, almost petrified nature of the passive Belladona. ...n *The Waste Land* she is arid, not sailing and 'wooing the very air'. Cleopatra had pretty dimpled boys 'like smiling Cupids' who become, in this chamber, ornaments of gold, inanimate. The dolphin is used in Shakespeare's play in association with Antony who is like the dolphin in both existing in *and* rising above his proper element. Very much a 'proper man', Antony rises out of the human element to become god-like in his capacity both in love and in war, though he is doomed to sink and be swallowed in his decadence. Here, in the claustrophobic boudoir, we have only a carved dolphin, vitality arrested in stone, 'swimming in sad light'. Where Cleopatra was a real queen in love as well as a gipsy in lust, touching a transcendency in her passion for Antony and dying for it, Belladona, in her suspended gesture of feminine vanity, gives no sense of passion. Her dialogue with the man, husband or lover, is without any real communication, even of her pampered senses. Cleopatra and the other African queen, Dido, were both placed by Dante in his Inferno and both die violently after their banquets of love. From Virgil's account in his *Aeneid* (Book I) of the welcoming and banqueting of Aeneas by Dido, comes the strange word *laquearia* (l. 82), the cupola into which the lamps and blazing torches flung their light, while Dido was becoming possessed with the God of Love. She, like the traditional whore of Babylon and the ill-fated Isolde, raises a golden cup to proclaim a toast to a love indissolubly linked with death. Dido actually burns to death on a funeral pyre so that there may be an intended link too between Belladona's domestic fire,

> Huge sea-wood fed with copper

and Dido's pyre on Carthage shore. The 'burning' at the end of *The Fire Sermon* also follows close on the reference to Carthage to which St. Augustine had later come, calling it a 'cauldron of unholy loves'.

Present with Cleopatra and Dido as a part of the portrait is Pope's Belinda from *The Rape of the Lock*, another lady of vanity, acidly defined and implicitly judged by her possessions:

> Puffs, powders, patches, Bibles, billet-doux.

It was perhaps from Pope's satiric portrait that Eliot takes the ironic trick of confusing dressing-table with altar to suggest the excesses of vanity. Belinda too gazes in a mirror where

> A heavenly image in the glass appears;
> To that she bends, to that her eyes she rears.
> The inferior priestess, at her altar's side,
> Trembling begins the sacred rites of Pride.

There is a hint of pseudo-sanctity and self-worship in the seven-branched candelabra and incense-like rising odours of Belladona's profane 'chapel-boudoir'. So too the traditional whore of Babylon is associated with the Apocalyptic candlestick in the *Book of Revelation*.

If the ghost of Cleopatra brings the 'serpent of old Nile' to mind, other snakes lurk here; in particular Keats' serpent-enchantress Lamia, whose sumptuous Corinthian banquet-chamber is echoed in several of the visual details. Lamia's 'glowing' banquet-hall has a faery-roof of 'fresh carved cedar mimicking a glade'. There is a feast laid out 'teeming with odours' and the serpent bride

> In pale contented sort of discontent
> Shut her chamber up, close, hushed and still.

This phrase may well have contributed, especially in its context of eerie magic, to the disturbing

> staring forms
> Leaned out, leaning, hushing the room enclosed.

Lamia's room is panelled and before each lucid panel stood

> A censer fed with myrrh and spiced wood,

as Belladona's fire is fed with sea-wood and copper. Above all, there is the same heavily charged mingling of the senses rendered in the description of mixed light and perfumes:

> fifty wreaths of smoke
> From fifty censers their light voyage took
> To the high roof, still mimicked as they rose
> Along the mirrored walls by twin clouds odorous.

Such a luxurious confusion is echoed in Eliot's lines 89–93. Lamia's erotic feast ends of course with the shattering of the spell and with death instead of marriage as consummation:

> Then Lamia breath'd death's breath

and Lycus, his arms 'empty of delight', dies too,

> And, in its marriage robe, the heavy body wound.

Belladona's is more of a living death, but any temporary spell spread by the luxury breaks as 'footsteps shuffled on the stair'. Her version of love in *The Waste Land* confirms the theme, present in a more Romantic form in the allusions to Lamia and to Tristan and Isolde in Part I, of an inevitable connection between love and death. In Burton's *Anatomy of Melancholy*, in a passage which Keats appended as a note to the last line of his poem, the philosopher who charges Lamia with being a serpent and distractor of virtuous youth, also says that

> All her furniture was, like Tantalus' gold, described by Homer, no substance but mere illusions.

It seems significant that all Belladona's sumptuous furniture too drops out of the scene once the stark dialogue with her man begins, becoming illusory when the naked nerves of the protagonists are exposed:

> 'I never know what you are thinking. Think.'
> I think we are in rats' alley.

The notion of décor *mimicking*, first a glade, then real light by mirrors, is twice repeated in the description of Lamia's hall. This and the notion of a serpent-temptress leads to the representation above Belladona's antique mantel. It, too, cheats with a *trompe l'œil* effect:

> As though a window gave upon the sylvan scene ...

This is the only glimpse of Paradise in this chamber, the phrase 'sylvan scene' having been used by Milton of the place where Adam and Eve enjoyed perfect, unfallen love. But the phrase comes in Book IV, line 140 at a point where the serpent-tempter is about to enter and destroy paradise. Moreover, Eliot steals the phrase to evoke first its proper context, already troubled, and then his new ironic one where it is applied not to Paradise but to the wood where Philomel was raped by Tereus. It is an effect of art too, a pseudo-window in a stuffy chamber; a paradise lost indeed.

Linked with Philomel and juxtaposed with the *femmes fatales* who descend from the whore of Babylon, all women who met violent deaths through passion, are the corresponding set of female victim figures, sufferers at the hands of lust and treachery. Juxtaposed with the allusions to the barge speech in *Antony and Cleopatra* are hints of Imogen's chamber from *Cymbeline*. In that play Iachimo is treacherously trying to prove that Imogen has been unfaithful to her husband, Posthumous, by giving so detailed and intimate an account of her bed-chamber that it must prove that he has spent a night there with her. The first detail he gives is of a tapestry of

> Proud Cleopatra, when she met her Roman
> And Cydnus swell'd above the banks.

Eliot seizes on this association of Imogen with the less innocent Cleopatra and mingles the details of the two contexts with virtuosity. Enobarbus describes Cleopatra's attendants:

> on each side her
> Stood pretty dimpled boys, like smiling Cupids.

Iachimo, describing the roof of Imogen's chamber says

> The roof of the chamber, with golden cherubims is fretted. Her andirons (I had forgot them) were two winking Cupids of silver. . . .

These two merge in Belladona's mirror, symbol of her vanity:

> where the glass
> Held up by standards wrought with fruited vines
> From which a golden Cupidon peeped out
> (Another hid his eyes behind his wing)

A further link between Belladona and the victim Philomel is subtly suggested via Imogen. Iachimo smuggles himself into her chamber in a trunk to gain his information and discovers that before sleeping she had been reading

> The Tale of Tereus, here the leaf's turn'd down
> Where Philomel gave up.

The irony of this is also clear in Eliot's context and underlies the connection between violence and suffering which is part of his sad analysis of reduced erotic love in *The Waste Land*. Shakespeare had made his Lucrece, too, invoke Philomel after her rape by Tarquin:

> Come, Philomel, that sing'st of ravishment,
> Make thy sad grove in my dishevell'd hair . . .

> For burthen-wise I'll hum on Tarquin still,
> While thou on Tereus descant'st better skill.

It would be possible to enumerate more sources for this dense portrait of the dual aspect of woman as seductress and victim. It is clear that in

this passage at least, the more one recognises, the fuller and more suggestive will it become. But it *is* a set-piece, in the pictorial manner, and it is
not necessary to an initial impression and understanding to have the
mind stocked with exactly the reading that went into Eliot's picture
any more than it is to have read obscure books of travel to respond to
The Ancient Mariner. The parallels and ironies are, moreover, fairly
clear when sources are recognised. But not all Eliot's allusions are of this
straight contributory kind nor do they operate in this manner, adding to
the dimensions of the portrait but only confirming its surface impression
of a sad, luxurious woman, victim and temptress in love.

Elsewhere even easy and familiar allusions such as those to Andrew
Marvell's *To his Coy Mistress* in *The Fire Sermon* can be far from simple
in their effect:

> But at my back in a cold blast I hear
> The rattle of the bones, and chuckle spread from ear to ear,

and later:

> But at my back from time to time I hear
> The sound of horns and motors.

Recognition comes primarily from the phrase 'But at my back' and
secondarily from a sense that the familiar rhythmic pattern of

> I alwaies hear
> Times winged Charriot hurrying near

is rudely broken by Eliot. In Marvell's poem the threat of time and
mortality is used to further the urgent plea of 'carpe diem' through
sexual love. Fear itself is made into an incentive and terror of mortality
is to be violently integrated with desire in the desperate

> Let us roll all our strength, and all
> Our sweetness, up into one Ball;
> And tear our pleasures with rough strife,
> Thorough the iron gates of Life.

The prevailing tone is defiant—'Now therefore'—and the appalling
glimpse of 'Desarts of vast Eternity' is fended off by the wilful assertion
of the present. But Eliot is embedding his theft in a very different
context, one in which disgust and terror are turned upon erotic love as
well as upon death and putrefaction. The Buddha's Fire Sermon, to which
the title alludes, counsels a withdrawal from the world of the senses,
as everything which assaults the senses is part of the fire of mortality.

Thus it is part of Eliot's attempt here to evoke disgust for what would normally constitute temptation, and, to Marvell, a means of emotional triumph over mortality. So he twice marries the phrase 'But at my back' bathetically to a new phrase, each time sardonically reducing the images of death and erotic love:

> in a cold blast I hear
> The rattle of the bones, and chuckle spread from ear to ear,

and later, following a reiteration of the rattling bones, now linked by sound association with the disgusting rat, we have white bodies naked and bones:

> Rattled by the rat's foot only, year to year.
> But at my back from time to time I hear
> The sound of horns and motors, which shall bring
> Sweeney to Mrs. Porter in the spring.

The grotesque charnel imagery may well have been suggested by Marvell's evocation of the grave in his poem, the grave where the worm tries

> That long preserv'd virginity.

But there is a difference in tone between his witty linking of sexuality and putrefaction and the more pained disgust of

> White bodies naked on the low damp ground
> And bones cast in a little low dry garret.

In Sweeney's grotesquely heralded rendezvous in the spring with Mrs. Porter, where the lines parody those of Day's *Parliament of Bees*, the sense parodies perhaps the amorous triumph of the ending of Marvell's poem. The sardonic 'from time to time' in the place of 'alwaies' is a measure of the difference of tone intended.

The force of this allusion is therefore very complicated; on the one hand, Eliot seems to want to steal wholesale the terror of mortality which Marvell evokes before defying it. The unaltered 'But at my back' establishes this, reminding us of the sense of a breathless race, of persecution. On the other hand, he clearly wishes to overturn the possibility of defiance of time which follows in Marvell's poem. His own poem is set in the 'desarts of vast eternity' and in the living grave of the 'unreal city'. He had overturned the sweet lyricism of Spenser's *Prothalamion* by painting a Thames littered not with marriage flower petals but with

> Silk handkerchiefs, cardboard boxes, cigarette ends
> Or other testimony of summer nights.

Just as his river becomes the setting of casual, anonymous sexual encounters, so here, he dissolves the possibility of erotic triumph in the insistence upon the charnel and by the bathos of Sweeney as horny lover in Mrs. Porter's house of pleasure.

The Marvell allusion became an object in a collage, torn from its context and roughly juxtaposed. We may see it, for example, as a milk bottle top. As such it may imply the whole bottle but that whole has only an ironic place in the new context. In thematic terms, sex in Eliot's *Waste Land* has become either a thwarted yearning (see ll. 35–42 and the response to the Third Command) or part of a living death, a charnel experience sharing nothing of the desperate exuberance of

> Let us roll all our strength, and all
> Our sweetness, up into one Ball.

This question of the shift of tone and emphasis leads to the more difficult one of the way in which irony is used in *The Waste Land*. Henry James[22] analysed what he calls the 'strength of applied irony' as

> being surely in the sincerities, the lucidities, the utilities that stand behind it. . . . It implies and projects the possible other case, the case rich and edifying where the actuality is pretentious and vain.

Very often in *The Waste Land*, with its allusion to past myths and lyrical poetry, we seem to have precisely this. So often it is the allusion, often in fragmentary form, that gives us the 'possible other case'. The ironic juxtaposition of what may seem rich and edifying with a reductive rather than a pretentious actuality throws a kind of two-way light, casting both doubt upon the possible other case and despair upon the sordid actual. Too many commentators on the poem have simplified this double effect and maintained that the chief function of Eliot's allusions to past myths and literature is to show that he is measuring a mean present against the vanished glories of a past for which he is, lyrically, sighing. Finding the present manifestations of lust, ennui and spiritual emptiness painful and disgusting, the poet, we are told, further degrades them by comparison with a Romantic past; Grail knight and maiden against gas-house, Tristan and Isolde, Cleopatra, Philomel, Ophelia, Spenser's nymphs, Elizabeth and Leicester, Ferdinand and Miranda against Sweeney and Mrs. Porter, the typist and her 'young man', Madame

[22] H. James, *The Art of the Novel*, Critical Prefaces by Henry James, ed. R. P. Blackmur (New York, 1934), p. 222.

Sosostris and Lil against Ezekiel and Tiresias. Because these figures are evoked lyrically, the poet must be expressing a regret for the past which is stronger than the parallel with the present which the irony would suggest. This seems to me to be a seriously mistaken view of how Eliot's allusions work. The process of history may have heightened vulgarity, the violated nightingale's song become ' "Jug Jug" to dirty ears', but there was nothing to be nostalgically regretted about the rape of Philomel, 'by the barbarous king so rudely forced'. Spenser's sweet nymphs are to be regretted in their fecund marriage context but Elizabeth and Leicester's gilded shell cannot conceal the idle and fruitless passion with which they drift 'past the Isle of Dogs', ironically enough towards

> The peal of bells
> White towers

suggestive of a sanctity from which they are excluded. Similarly, when Eliot invites us in his Notes to make parallels between Baudelaire's

> Fourmillante cité, cité pleine de rêves,
> Où le spectre en plein jour raccroche le passant

and the crowd of lost souls in Dante's *Inferno* undone by death and sighing and his own

> Unreal City,
> Under the brown fog of a winter dawn,
> A crowd flowed over London Bridge, so many,
> I had not thought death had undone so many.
> Sighs, short and infrequent, were exhaled,
> And each man fixed his eyes before his feet . . .

it is because he wants to invest his own vision of a crowd of London workers with a spectral dimension, probably inspired by their appearance in the brown fog. He persuades us by the parallels of his conviction that their anonymous flow and sighs of boredom and downcast look amount to a form of damnation or a living death, ghost-like, unreal.

A different kind of problem arises with those allusions, usually less fragmentary, to narrative and dramatic works. When the allusion is torn from a context of character and action, which, if we recognise the source at all, is bound to come to mind, the memory may again set up irrelevant associations. A crucial example of this is the famous allusion to Hieronymo in Kyd's *The Spanish Tragedy* at the very end of *The Waste Land*:

> These fragments I have shored against my ruins
> Why then Ile fit you. Hieronymo's mad againe.

This is momentously followed by the repetition of the sacred command of the Thunder and the words of ineffable peace:

> Shantih shantih shantih.

Hieronymo in Kyd's play, in offering to 'fit' or suit the court by managing an entertainment in which the courtiers will act their parts in many languages, is in fact fitting or suiting his own, half-insane plan of revenge for the murder of his son. He is resorting, first to apparent, and then to real insanity; law and order are lost. He is moreover attempting to use a play, a form of art to restore a more cogent form of reality in a totally corrupt world. As he says,

> When I was young, I gave my mind
> And plied myself to fruitless poetry.

A little later when the play has begun and two of the actors have been stabbed not in show but in fact, the action is interrupted by Hieronymo's desperate 'showing' of reality, the putrefying corpse of his son whom he had found 'hanging on a tree'. Foiled of a distracted attempt to hang himself, Hieronymo cries:

> But never shalt thou force me to reveal
> The thing which I have vowed inviolate.
> And therefore, in despite of all my threats,
> Pleas'd with their deaths, and eas'd with their revenge,
> First take my tongue, and afterwards my heart . . .

and he violently pulls out his own tongue.

If we know this much of the Kyd context many details begin to strike us as relevant to Eliot's poem and the juxtaposition of Tiresias with Hieronymo seems less arbitrary. Since Madame Sosostris' admission in Part I—

> I do not find
> The Hanged Man—

there has lurked in the poem the elusive image of the hanged man. He may be Stetson's planted corpse and becomes by implication the sacrificial hanged god of fertility cults and the crucified Christ. The penultimate fragment 'O swallow swallow' has just reminded us of the legend of Philomel and Procne, of violated and transformed womanhood, which has also run throughout the text. The poet had longed to be as the swallow, migratory bird of hope and legendarily supposed to have uttered its cry 'console, console' at the Cross. The sister bird Philomel had had her tongue torn out to prevent her revealing her brutal rape by Tereus and had been rewarded in metamorphosis by becoming bird of 'inviolable voice'. There is thus a grotesque parallel with the avenger's tearing out of his own tongue to keep the secret which he has vowed 'inviolate'. Philomel had woven a *peplus* to reveal her story of undoing, as Hieronymo had demonstrated the truth in a contrived play in which the actors spoke in hidden voices, unknown languages. This extraordinary coalescence of details would seem to suggest that here at least Eliot *is* wishing to invoke the context of his fragment in considerable detail. But there are still many problems.

In actually quoting the sub-title on the frontispiece of the 1615 edition, 'Hieronymo's mad againe', reminding us that in the end Hieronymo is mad indeed, violently seeking self-destruction, is Eliot suggesting that distraction and madness underlie the end of his poem? Written as it is in several languages, its final message of peace and benediction is delivered in what is, for most of us, an 'unknown tongue', Sanskrit. In particular, may he be alluding by implication to Hieronymo's dismissal of poesy, art, as fruitless in the quest to achieve order and clarity out of chaos and injustice? This would reduce the force of the poet's longing for an inviolable voice in the midst of gross suffering and desolate ruins. Does the grotesque paralleling of tongueless Hieronymo with Philomel undermine any suggestion of the survival of art as a transcendent voice? Certainly the torn fragments of art in different tongues used to shore against ruins of civilisations and cultures, the falling towers, might suggest this. On the other side of the case there is a promise in the play's epilogue that Hieronymo's ghost will find peace. We have a hint that the whole context *is* relevant as Eliot's own Note refers us to the play entire, not to the place from which the phrase is taken. Also, Eliot was at that time steeped in Elizabethan and Jacobean tragedy. It is perhaps a weakness of Eliot's allusive method, particularly when he is using narrative or dramatic sources, that his own context does not define quite clearly enough how much of the original is being implied, whether straightforwardly or ironically. In the case of 'Hieronymo' a decision to take the original context into account may quite radically affect our notion of the complex tone and purport of the ending.

The *Spanish Tragedy* allusions are at least single and localised. It is even more difficult when, as in the case of Eliot's snatchings from *The Tempest*, the references are repeated and sustained to form part of an atmospheric and thematic pattern.[23] The first of these, the line from Ariel's song,

> Those are pearls that were his eyes

follows immediately on Madame Sosostris' discovery of her consultant's card, 'the drowned Phoenician sailor'. The idea of drowning is paramount in the mind of the shipwrecked Ferdinand in *The Tempest*. He believes his beloved father drowned and is interrupted in his grief by Ariel's song of sea-change, 'Full fathom five thy father lies', a song of the changing into coral and pearl of bone and eye, a bitter-sweet transformation. In its context in Shakespeare's play, the song precedes the first encounter of Ferdinand with Miranda, a quester with his maiden, a miraculous 'love at first sight' induced by Prospero's magic art. While Ferdinand exclaims:

> The ditty does remember my drowned father.
> This is no mortal business

Prospero is bidding his daughter to look upon her destined lover: 'The fringed curtain of thy eye advance'. But Eliot's exclamatory 'Look', following immediately on 'Those are pearls that were his eyes,' if it is retrospective, must either refer to the sea-changed eyes, or to the image of the drowned man itself, the Phoenician sailor, whose descent into the deep sea-swell and picked bones are to form a whole section—(IV)— later in the poem. Even if we did not know from Eliot's Note that Ferdinand is not wholly separate from the Phoenician sailor, we are well aware of the irony of alluding to Shakespeare's romantic and semi-mystical moment in which grief at a temporary loss is to be largely assuaged by the discovery of erotic love. It is a far cry from Shakespeare's island to Madame Sosostris' sordid parlour. If on the other hand her 'Look!' points forward, it is to a woman, but to Belladona, the Lady of the Rocks. Where Shakespeare's Ferdinand is the clear survivor of the wreck, Eliot's fleeting young male figure is to fear drowning, whether we understand it literally, as with Phlebas, or in a metaphoric sense of passional waters. Shakespeare's young hero can greet Miranda as 'O you wonder', but Belladona, devious Lady of situations, stale seductress,

[23] See note on p. 38.

is the very antithesis of the innocence which anticipates a 'brave new world'. Any parallel with *The Tempest* is, it seems, ironic and complicated in its ironies. In *A Game of Chess* some of *The Tempest* images are retained in the 'drowning' of the senses and in the rats' alley 'where the dead men lost their bones', in ways more horrific than by the sea's corrosion. The memory of 'Those are pearls that were his eyes' haunts the uncommunicative lover's consciousness in the form now of the degenerate and despairingly comic 'Shakespeherian Rag'. In *The Fire Sermon* Ferdinand re-appears, in person now, identified with the figure fishing on the banks of the dull canal:

> Musing upon the king my brother's wreck,
> And on the king my father's death before him.

He is musing not upon the sea-change, but upon the ghastliness of mortality and the link between sexuality and physical decay and death:

> White bodies naked on the low damp ground
> And bones cast in a little low dry garret,

Eliot's change of 'father' to 'brother' has puzzled critics, leading to speculation about a hermit brother of the Fisher King. But the most important thing about the change is surely that in *The Waste Land* we cannot make a total identification between Shakespeare's original Ferdinand and Eliot's derived but complex and shadowy figure. He is like Shakespeare's Prince of Naples in brooding over a lost father but expands beyond Ferdinand's narrative position by mourning a brother too, also a king, a younger man like Phlebas, figuring a 'death', real or metaphoric of the youthful questing generation. This generation includes Ferdinand himself, and is possibly to be extended further by the association of 'brother' with the 'frère' in Baudelaire's line:

> You! hypocrite lecteur!—mon semblable,—mon frère!

'Brother' expands till it touches the reader's self which is being mourned by his 'semblable', the poet.

Whatever we understand by this change in reference, as with the notorious change from wolf to dog in the allusion (line 74) to Webster's dirge from *The White Devil* (explications range from Cleanth Brooks' humanitarianism to DOG as an acrostic for GOD, a displaced person in *The Waste Land*!), it is clear that the original context, both its narrative detail and its general atmosphere, is only invoked to be modified or

E

extended. Recognition is only the first, crude stage in our response. The line spoken by Ferdinand as he hears Ariel's magic music and rightly takes it to be unearthly and of spiritual import is inserted into *The Fire Sermon* between the typist's gramophone record, itself reminiscent of the 'Shakespeherian Rag' of *A Game of Chess*, and 'the pleasant whining of a mandoline' which the protagonist can sometimes distinguish from the clatter and chatter of a fishmen's lounge bar. Whilst this music is pleasant and to be distinguished from the canned music put on by 'automatic' hand, some commentators have sentimentalised this section speaking of an 'organic' fishing community in the city with its musical bar and splendid church. The music is in fact described as 'whining' and the sigh 'O City, city' seems to have a tone of regret, almost anguish, for the glimpses of beauty, music and white and gold, are fleeting and inexplicable. We are in the heart of London, the commercial city (the fishmen are fish merchants and catchers) an area containing the Cannon Street Hotel, and the typist's flat, the 'unreal city' of the poem's opening section.

The music which crept by Shakespeare's Ferdinand as he sat grieving on a bank which Eliot changes to the dull canal 'round behind the gashouse', heralded that play's transformation of a tangle of treacheries, death and misery into a pattern of forgiveness, redemption, rebirth and rejoicing. Such transformation is hinted at in the change of eyes to pearls, symbolic of wisdom and purity. But in *The Waste Land*, where re-birth is wearily sought but never found, the sea-change itself may not get beyond the macabre and naturalistic 'Davie Jones' sense of flesh into pearl, itself a diseased growth in oysters. The glimpses of beauty have no transcendent significance here, only a wistful, transient flash. Our memory of the true 'Tempest' atmosphere is not however irrelevant, since it becomes a measure of the loss endured by the inhabitants of the waste. In this case the play's themes are invoked precisely to show their essential distance from the ironic new context of the snatched allusions.

III

Having discussed the different kinds of problem which arise in the case of fragmentary allusions, straight and ironic, to lyrical, dramatic and narrative sources, I want in this final section to discuss three sources and influences upon Eliot's poem which seem less important for their verbal and local contribution than for the much more subtle and pervasive part they play in the overall tone and balance of emphasis of the whole poem.

The first of these sources are the Old Testament Hebrew Prophets Isaiah, Ezekiel and Jeremiah. The warning voices of Ezekiel and the preacher of Ecclesiastes lie behind ll. 19–30 and Ezekiel's 'Valley of dry bones' behind the 'rattle of the bones' in *The Fire Sermon*. In Part V the wanderings in the desert are reminiscent of the Exodus from the Sinai wilderness where Moses struck water with his rod. The wind blowing across it also recalls Ezekiel's prophecy of the restoration of the scattered tribes of Israel. These allusions have long been familiar but it was not until Florence Jones'[24] article 'T. S. Eliot Among the Prophets' that the claim was made that the influence of the prophets is 'paramount in Eliot's poem'. Miss Jones demonstrates convincingly that there are further and detailed parallels between the prophets' images and those of Eliot's *Waste Land*. His 'rock' (see ll. 25 and 324–58) reminds us of the Rock of Israel, the God of the prophets who is both a refuge and a stumbling block. There is no water, such as Moses struck, among Eliot's dry rock. In *Isaiah* 2:10 rock is found in conjunction with dust from which it is a refuge but not yet a salvation. Jeremiah, denouncing and lamenting the degeneration of seventh-century Judah, uses terms very similar to those chosen by Eliot to decry the doomed state of twentieth-century civilisation. Both suggest that the absence of God is a time of burning, both in its sense of lust, of purgatorial purification and destructive judgement, the 'falling towers and cities'. Judah's wells are empty and her cisterns broken (cf. l. 384); her crops fail too and her people are barren. The prophet also uses the figure of Judah as an unfaithful, defiled bride, and a choice vine become fruitless. In both cases one has a similar pattern of personalities; in *Jeremiah* God is the King married to his land, an erring faithless queen, with the prophet to warn and mediate between them. There is also in the prophets the promise of a deliverer, a Son of Man, who will restore the land, both its morality and its fertility. This deliverer may have an equivalent in the quester figure in *The Waste Land*. If he succeeds live shoots will spring again and the desolate city be rebuilt. The restored city is envisaged by Ezekiel as built round the temple with the River of Life issuing from below its threshold:

And wherever the river goes every living creature which swarms will live, and there will be very many fish.

Isaiah (33:20–1) also says God will be 'unto us a place of broad rivers and

[24] F. Jones, 'T. S. Eliot among the Prophets', *American Literature* (1966), pp. 285–301.

streams'. The breaking of the cords of the tent, or tabernacle, is part of the desolation. These parallel images cannot be fortuitous though I cannot go on to agree with Miss Jones that just as the Hebrew prophets are obliquely foretelling the coming of the true deliverer, not the pagan Phoenician cults but the Hanged Man, Christ the true Rock, so Eliot 'is insisting that God is our deliverer'. It seems quite clear that this possibility, like the missed opportunity of romantic love in the Hyacinth garden, is tentatively explored in the hallucinatory lines 359–65. But the quester-figure never becomes unequivocally a deliverer in *The Waste Land*, whereas his mere 'coming' will be enough to the prophets. The hooded third person, if he is a deliverer, remains unidentified just as Madame Sosostris fails to find the Hanged Man. If, as Miss Jones suggests, the response to the third command (ll. 418–22) owes something to *Isaiah* (33:23) where Israel's unworthiness is seen in the image of a boat with loose tackle and unstable mast and to Jeremiah's iteration of the Lord's promise that

I will give them a heart to know that I am the Lord . . . for they shall return to me with their whole heart

it also owes much to the erotic strain in the poem. There is a world of difference between the mood and tone of 'would have' and the God of Israel's firm 'I will' and 'they shall'.

As with some of the 'narrative threads' discussed earlier, any singling out of even such a sustained string of allusions and sources will almost inevitably lead to a false or at least unbalanced account of the poem.

Eliot used the Hebrew prophets, as he used the Fisher King and fertility cult material to extend the time dimension of his poem. Like the myths, the prophetic denunciations of degeneration, threats of desolation and promises of restoration are relevant to his analysis of a barren modern world. But part of this world's predicament is precisely that prophecy itself is degraded. There have always been false prophets, but in Eliot's *Waste Land* there is no evidence of an Ezekiel or a Jeremiah to counteract the sordid commercial game, playing on fear, carried out by Madame Sosostris and Mrs. Equitone. Even these phonies feel insecure in their position:

One must be so careful these days.

Tiresias, the pagan prophet, is present too, but unlike the lone voices in the wilderness, seems to have participated in the degeneration himself, having twice changed sex, 'foresuffered all' and even 'walked among the lowest of the dead'. Blind now, he has paradoxically become the compassionate 'voyeur' but his voice never reaches those he sees, nor has he apparently any message of hope of deliverance for them, just as Madame Sosostris could only warn, not advise, and the Cumean Sibyl was longing for her own death. It is not that Eliot ironically dismisses the solemn tones of the Hebrew prophets having invoked them; it is rather that it is their tone of dire warning, and not their promise of deliverance that he wants to contribute to his own tone. The 'something different', the 'fear in a handful of dust' which he shows does not amount to a healthy 'fear of the Lord' forming a positive turning point for the wayward tribes. Rather it is a terrifying vision of mortality, of living death and aridity which issues in commands not from the God of Israel but from an Eastern Thunder God; commands which have all been disobeyed and form therefore a code for further trial rather than a Messianic promise of deliverance. They do issue in a blessing which casts peace over the fragments, but it is pronounced in a sad rather than confidently exultant tone.

Contributing a note of more elegiac sadness to this tone, is another of what I have called the all-pervasive or 'atmospheric' allusions which underlie the text. Like the allusions to the Old Testament prophets, this source is locally explicit, but only in Part I of the poem, where it forms the lyrical framework to the episode in the Hyacinth garden. Stravinsky[25] records Eliot's life-long passion for Wagner's music: *Tristan und Isolde* was 'one of the most passionate experiences of his life'. The appearance of Tristan and Isolde and of the Rhine maidens of *Gotterdämmerung* in *The Waste Land* are both important to the theme and form a strong lyrical element in the complex range of tones on which the poem is based. The Tristan legend itself contains much ancient mythological material in common with the erotic element in the Grail legends. Tristan's original and his later sword wounds require the healing powers for which Isolde, betrothed to the ageing king (like some versions of the Grail maiden), is famed. This has a clear link with Eliot's use of the legends of questing knight, wounded king and redeeming maiden. The sword and the cup from which the love potion, replacing deadly poison, is drunk take up the sexual symbolism of the Grail lance

[25] Igor Stravinsky and Robert Craft, *Themes and Episodes* (New York, 1966), pp. 124–6. It is worth noting that Eliot published two articles by T. Sturge Moore on the literary uses of the Tristan legend in *The Criterion* 1922 (Vol. I, no. 1 and Vol. II, no. 2).

and cup, male and female. The tragic presence of adultery and betrayal undermine the possibility of love's fulfilment, so fitting into Eliot's treatment of the theme of the failure of human love. In the opera an ecstatic garden love-scene ends in the violence of a sword fight with a treacherous friend. Later, wounded again, Tristan lies, Hyacinthus-like, upon a bank of flowers yearning both for death and for the advent by sea of Isolde who has already become an intrinsic part of the consummation both of love and of death. When she comes Tristan rises, opening his wound fatally and, again like Hyacinth and Adonis, expires in a torrent of blood. These general parallels, plus the further associations of sea voyages with the discovery, consummation and loss of love, serve Eliot's theme, but beyond this, his quotations from Wagner's libretto surely add too a purely lyrical sound effect to the poem. They frame the garden scene and pin-point the two moods of expectation undermined by fear and desperate yearning and desolation which mark his own love episode. Eliot seems here to be aspiring almost to 'poésie pure', to sound above sense, hence perhaps his willingness to leave the fragments in German. It is the evocative musical setting of the songs, sung by a sailor and a piping shepherd and epitomising the passionate mode of the opera, that is relevant rather than the intricacies of the situation at the precise moments when they are sung. These intricacies can indeed distract. Isolde is being unwillingly ferried towards an agèd and unwanted husband and is angry at Tristan, commissioned to bring her, for his slaying of her former betrothed and for his duplicity in disguising his identity when seeking a cure for his own wound. She feels alone, betrayed and insulted and takes even this innocent sailor's song as an insult to herself. But the music here is already moving towards the drama of the love-potion and the lovers' consequent death-tainted passion. The second quotation, taken from the midst of the last act as Tristan lies wounded and yearning is both verbally and musically evocative of desolation. The shepherd set to watch for her boat can still see nothing and so continues his sad tune, bleakly and mournfully played on a single instrument. Later the ship is indeed to come and the tune to change though Isolde brings not a cure but their death and the passionate ecstasy of the *Liebestod* is subsumed in transfiguration.

It is almost as if Eliot were trying to evoke background music here, a sound dimension of a peculiarly passionate kind for what is the uniquely passionate moment of his poem, missed or marred as it turns out to be. The *Liebestod* theme, the link between yearning erotic love and treachery and death, becomes a further instance of Eliot's making parallels to point a difference. The wounded Tristan, like weary Tiresias and the Cumean Sibyl, longs for death as a release from what he describes as his soul's 'parching ache'. Day and light burn and sear him. He longs for night and insensibility. He suffers perhaps an erotic version of the desert experience of Eliot's Section V. Significantly, Eliot's second quotation comes before the ache is assuaged in the consummation of death. But Eliot's lovers are far from this intensity, either its sufferings or delights. When they approach it at all they fail, miss the moment:

> your heart would have responded.

Instead they survive to descend into a limbo condition of lonely boredom, indifference and hysteria:

> 'What shall we do tomorrow?
> 'What shall we ever do?'

and

> 'Well now that's done: and I'm glad it's over.'

Thus their poetic distance from Tristan and Isolde seems measureless but Eliot's incorporation of Wagner's atmosphere into his text serves as a reverberating reminder of what 'might have been', blending elegiac sadness with the weariness of tone and ironies of his love episodes. The allusions are meant to operate far beyond their local context in Part I.

It is even possible for a reader familiar with Wagner's opera to feel a tacit allusion, not textually sign-posted but emotionally intended, to Isolde's final words, 'Are they gentle aerial waves ringing out clearly, surging round me? Are they ocean waves of blissful fragrance? As they seethe and roar about me, shall I breathe, shall I listen? Shall I drink of them, plunge beneath them, breathe my life away in sweet scents? In the heaving swell, in the resounding echoes, in the universal stream of world-breath, to drown, to founder, unconscious—utmost rapture.' None of the drownings in the poem attain such rapture and Eliot's symbolic landscape, with its broken images, roots that clutch, and long-delayed shower breaking over Himavant, seems to resist surrender to any Jungian 'universal stream of the world', actual or metaphoric. The poem does not deny its existence but the whole could almost be described as a lament for individual man's loss of relation to its flow: 'Your hand *would have* responded' and, in the drafts, the guilt-tinged sorrow of the isolated ego expressed in 'I left without you/Clasping empty hands I sit upon the shore.' But, I would maintain, Isolde's passionate alternative *is* invoked like the true Grail encounter as part of the poet's registration of dismay at the 'handful of dust'.

In a poem where narrative threads are so tenuous, often deliberately hidden, the reliance on the power of an allusion, especially to a musical work, to last and reverberate beyond the local context and form part of our total emotional response becomes a vital part of the poetic technique.

Nothing could be further from this tone of Romantic ecstasy than my last example of a general, atmospheric contributor to Eliot's poem, the *Satyricon* of Petronius, thought to be a favourite of Nero, a recorder in satire of that period's decadence. Eliot used a quotation from the *Satyricon* as an epigraph to his poem and in *The Sacred Wood*, 1920, which also has an epigraph taken from the *Satyricon* he remarked 'We think more highly of Petronius than our grandfathers'. This led people to question the extent and nature of Eliot's knowledge of Petronius and recently Herbert Howarth[27] established that Eliot attended a Harvard course on the Roman Novel given by Clifford H. Moore in 1908–9. It was at Harvard too in 1911–12 that Eliot attended Charles Lanman's Sanskrit class and probably acquired the Sanskrit material later used in the poem and began his study of Indian philosophy and Buddhism. But he would have been studying the Roman writer at a period when the influence of another 'decadent', Laforgue, was beginning to be formative. Two scholars in particular have suggested detailed parallels between *The Waste Land* and the *Satyricon*, Helen Bacon[28] and F. N. Lees.[29] Both convincingly suggest general parallels of theme and tone between the two sardonic visions of contemporary decadence, empty pleasure-seeking and overthrow of traditional values. Both also pursue parallels of detail which are often more dubious. Phlebas' drowning in Section IV, which is itself a re-working in more intense form of Eliot's earlier *Dans le Restaurant*, ll. 25–31, can also be related to the drowning of the trader Lichas in the shipwreck episode (*Satyricon*, 114–15). The commercial phrase 'profit and loss' forms a link. This death by water is grotesquely

[27] H. Howarth, *Notes on some figures behind T. S. Eliot* (London, 1965), pp. 70–2.

[28] H. Bacon, 'The Sibyl in the Bottle', *Virginia Quarterly Review*, XXXIV (1958), pp. 262–76.

[29] F. N. Lees, '*Mr Eliot's Sunday Morning, Satura*, Petronius and *The Waste Land*', in *T. S. Eliot, The Man and his Work*, ed. Allen Tate (London, 1967), pp. 345–54.

rather than tragically described by Petronius. But it draws from the anti-hero Encolpius an elegy which, though it begins almost as a bombastic parody of a formal elegy such as the group devoted to drowned seamen in *The Greek Anthology*, suddenly changes tone to become a frantic cry against mortality and ruin. This fear of mortality and the preoccupation with death also underlies the orgiastic feast given by the freeman Trimalchio which turns at last into a mock funeral feast at which he pronounces his own epitaph. It is this Trimalchio who tells the story of the shrivelled Sibyl taunted by boys, which Eliot uses as epigraph. The grim joke of being condemned to everlasting life without the gift of youth fits exactly Petronius' kind of humour. The theme of a quest for fertility in *The Waste Land* is satirically paralleled in the *Satyricon* in the anti-hero's picaresque quest to restore his lost potency, taken from him by the wrath of Priapus, as Odysseus was pursued by the wrath of Poseidon. This quest leads him and his companions, after their ship-wreck, to the city of Croton, a city which had once been great and renowned as a place of luxury but, by Petronius' day, had suffered devastation in the Pyrrhic and Hannibalic wars. Its population had been transferred *en bloc* elsewhere, leaving it a 'ghost-town' of squatters. It is tempting to identify them with the 'hooded hordes' of displaced wanderers and the 'red sullen faces . . . from doors of mudcracked houses' in Eliot's poem and to see Croton as yet another facet of his 'unreal city' and 'falling towers'.

Encolpius and his companions, like Eliot's desert travellers for whom

Sweat is dry and feet are in the sand

arrive

in montem sudantes conscendimus,

drenched in sweat, and are told on enquiry that Croton is now a city where 'literature and the arts go utterly unhonoured' and where there are no natural fathers or naturally bred sons because the whole town is given over to legacy-hunters. The stay at Croton thus becomes a comic satire on the wiles of unscrupulous spongers and cheats. There is a possibility that whilst we may be on the road to Emmaus, the road of Christian ascetic pilgrimage in Part V of the poem, we are simultaneously on the road to Croton. Like the listed cities which bridge pagan and Christian cultural centres:

> Jerusalem Athens Alexandria
> Vienna London

Croton is 'unreal' both in its decline and in the period of decadent luxury which preceded its 'falling towers'.

Interesting though such parallels may be—and they are unlikely to be entirely accidental—the chief contribution of Petronius' work to Eliot's poem lies more in its literary genre and tone. It provides one link in the historic chain which Eliot forges between *The Waste Land*, Jacobean and Elizabethan literature, Dante and the classical epics of Virgil and Homer which lie behind Petronius' satirical imitations. This chain can be observed in miniature behind lines 293-4, where a Thames daughter says:

> Highbury bore me. Richmond and Kew
> Undid me . . .

echoing, first, Dante's unhappy Pia who cried in *Purgatorio* (V. 133)

> Siena mi fe, disfecemi Maremma,

and secondly a line traditionally supposed to have been uttered by Virgil on his deathbed:

> Mantua me genuit, Calabri rapuere tenet nunc
> Parthenope.

Virgil's undoing is by death, which occurred in Calabria; Pia's undoing involved sexual betrayal and death and happened at Maremma. The Thames daughter's undoing was also sexual and has led to the state of living death.

Both Miss Bacon and F. N. Lees point out that Petronius sardonically juxtaposes his anti-hero with the epic adventurers Aeneas and Odysseus by echoing and sometimes parodying Virgil's style and, behind it, that of Homer. He also works into his writing several comic discussions on the decline and abuses of rhetoric and 'high' literary styles so that on one level the work becomes a self-conscious satire on literary endeavour. Miss Bacon suggests that in Petronius, as in Eliot

> embedded in the language of a degenerate present is an echo from a
> world where passions are dignified and noble

and that

the reader is torn between the suggestion that the past, unlike the present, had dignity and meaning, and the horrible possibility that the past and present are one, that, under the fine language, the heroes of epic and mythology were rogues, tramps and sots, like Encolpius and his friends.

It may well be that it is partly from Petronius that Eliot developed his own ambiguous use of the past. By incorporating literary fragments, by quotation and by the near-parody of deliberate misquotation, he can evoke in his readers exactly this double possibility (see above, pp. 60–61). The past is *both* superficially unlike *and* essentially like the present.

Another almost accidental debt to Petronius may be to the fragmentary form in which the poem accidentally exists. Though its broken narrative threads and episodes cut off mid-stream to be followed by others apparently unconnected were no part of his intention (it is thought that the original *Satyricon* had 38 books), the fragmentary form may well have impressed Eliot and remained in his mind as an influence when he came to write a poem in which, even before Pound's excisions, narrative links are deliberately buried and the reader has to rely upon thematic organisation. Petronius's style, the brilliant display of imitations and parodies, ranging from gutter slang to mocking flights of rhetoric, intensifies this fragmentary effect which may be latent in any picaresque work. Similarly, in *The Waste Land* the abrupt changes of mood and idiom are achieved partly by the rapid adoption of quite different stylistic masks:

> *Oed' und leer das Meer*
> Madame Sosostris, famous clairvoyante,
> Had a bad cold.

So I would argue that it is primarily through a general debt to Petronius' style and to his tone which combines extravagant comedy with an underlying sense of fear which must be shrugged away, that Eliot is able to invoke the scurrilous world of the *Satyricon* as a counterpoint to the graver worlds of Grail mythology, Augustine's Christian asceticism, High Romantic love and dire Prophetic doom. It is only one of the many filters through which he wants his own contemporary world to be viewed. The link is the quest form which embraces the picaresque adventures of Encolpius, the Grail knights and the shadowy journeyer through *The Waste Land*. Above all, in Petronius as in Eliot, there is a skin of sharp ironic comedy stretched over a terror of moral anarchy and mortality. This terror is never far from the two works' surfaces. It breaks the skin at Trimalchio's feast and during the elegy over Lichas' body. In *The Waste Land* it is more all-pervasive. Both writers project worlds where the attempt to overthrow all former values, and the cultural forms which enshrine them, leave people with no option but to pursue blind appetite. They suffer the resultant boredom and need for artificial stimulants and distractions from the fact of death. In Petronius' tone defiant laughter prevails where in Eliot the despair is given fuller play. The epigraph contains a wry form of comedy, the sick joke that the Sibyl cannot die and finds the elixir of eternal mortal life a burden.

If the reader is able to detect this subtle comic tone and hold it simultaneously with the solemn warning and the passionate erotic yearning invoked from the Hebrew prophets and from Wagner's *Tristan* music, he will have approached the real purpose and reward for studying Eliot's sources.

† *APPENDIX*

Background Music in 'The Waste Land'

One of the most striking leaps of idiom in the poem comes when the typist, after her seduction,

> smoothes her hair with automatic hand,
> And puts a record on the gramophone.

This is part of a general attempt on Eliot's part to counterpoint two kinds of musical idiom in his text to parallel the counterpointing of poetic languages. Against the ragtime now popular in jazz-age London, and already familiar to him from his Harvard days, he set the heightened operatic lyricism of Wagner, the magical music invoked by Shakespeare in *The Tempest* and his admired Stravinsky. The Shakespearian rag that floats into *A Game of Chess* has been identified[30] as a hit song of 1912 and

---

[30] Bruce R. McElderry, Jr., *American Quarterly*, IX (1957), pp. 185-6.

the appendices of *They All Played Ragtime* (London, 1958) by Rudi Blesh and Harriet Janis yield a fascinating list of *Waste Land* rag titles: That Futuristic Rag, That International Rag, Operatic Rag, St. Louis Rag, Ophelia Rag, Valhalla Rag, Hyacinth Rag and even Possum Rag—the latter discounting any theory of Zeitgeist coincidence. These all date from 1911–12, and Stravinsky had followed his *Rite of Spring* with pieces influenced by rag music, the ragtime in *The Soldier's Tale*, the *Ragtime for Eleven Instruments* and *Piano Rag Music*. Like *doing voices* this element of musical experiment in *The Waste Land* aligns Eliot with a consciously international avant-garde movement in art which gave him freedom boldly to allude in one breath to Petronius and the Holy Grail while inviting us to hear the flip syncopated rhythm of

> That Shakesperean rag,—
> Most intelligent, very elegant,
> That old classical drag

against such examples of the classical drag as Isolde's last, passionately questioning notes of terror and ecstasy in Act V of *Tristan und Isolde*.

3. Hints and Guesses

I

> Out of these scatter'd Sibyl's leaves
> Strange Prophecies my Phancy weaves

In his touching preface to Valerie Eliot's beautiful facsimile and transcript of the original drafts of *The Waste Land*,[31] Pound, the poem's self-styled midwife, obliquely suggests that the unearthing of these long-scattered leaves may prove a mixed blessing. He is thankful they are found but adds, 'The occultation of *The Waste Land* m.s. is pure Henry James.' The hard moral lesson delivered to the literary critic and bio-grapher of James's *The Aspern Papers* is that his quest for Jeffrey Aspern's love letters ends in a bitter and humbling revelation of his own human inadequacies rather than in the grand literary-biographical revelation

[31] *The Waste Land: A Facsimile and Transcript of the Original Drafts including the Annotations of Ezra Pound* edited by Valerie Eliot (London, 1971).

expected. No one interested in Eliot's poem will want to deny the fascination of this new textual material, but the temptation of blending bibliographical with biographical discovery to foist a *new* interpretation on the poem or a drastic revaluation of its status should be resisted.

Two stale and heretical accounts of *The Waste Land* are already being revived; first, that it is a covert biographical 'confession' of marital misery and second, that it is the pretentiously and wilfully disguised narrative poem of an aridly clever poet. This new volume will undoubtedly be brought in *evidence* to support the kind of readings which some critics have long wanted to impose upon its often startlingly discontinuous form. The shock juxtaposition of scenes and the shifts of tone and intensity which so colour one's sense of *The Waste Land* are much less marked a feature of the more diffuse and sprawling original drafts. For all this, however, it seems much less certain that the nature and status of the poem will be seriously altered when the excitement has died down and the new material has been critically assimilated. Its most vital contribution will be the interpretative hints and confirmation of previous guesses to be outlined in the second part of this chapter.

The notion that the received text conceals some clue and merely awaits critical reassemblage has long bedevilled criticism, as has the view that its fragmentary nature is an act of deliberate obscurantism or, at most, a random effect brought about by Pound's editorial interventions. For years, it has been hinted and hoped that the discovery of the drafts would confirm such suspicions and dispel the poem's sybilline mysteries. While a careful analysis of the new material does testify, as Eliot always believed it would, to Pound's good taste and genius, it neither makes *The Waste Land* Pound's poem, nor does it reveal that it had at any stage been narrative or overtly confessional either in matter or in structure. The weakness of the verse in the poorer parts and the uneven, diffuse form of the total draft confirm Eliot's memory that the *Ur* Waste Land was just as structureless but in a more futile way.[32] Pound's major contribution is to have distinguished bad from good, flaccid from crisp verse and, by excision and some reordering of parts, to have tightened rather than reformed a basic structure.

Valerie Eliot's quotations from Eliot's letters of the period articulate more clearly some of the feelings and pressures that generated the poem. Their patterning in verse can now be traced through three stages,[33]

[32] See above pp. 15–16.   [33] See above p. 9.

Eliot's own working at his text, Pound's further tinkerings and Eliot's reactions, not always submissive, to these.

Of this first, and perhaps most vital, stage the new material gives us only glimpses.[34] In the drafts of *The Fire Sermon*, especially the apostrophe to the City which culminates in lines 257–65 of the received text, we can really see Eliot himself at work in the act of composition and correction. But elsewhere, what he was sending to Pound may well have gone through earlier stages and drafts that remain lost, so that, for all their fascination, these sheets can never precisely establish the dates and stages of composition of all the individual sections of the poem. More important, they cannot collectively reveal the exact chronology of Eliot's own attempts to order and arrange the whole. That he planned to have *Gerontion* as a preface and to use some of the other poems included in Valerie Eliot's volume, between the *sections*, confirms the impression that it was indeed Pound who established finally that *The Waste Land* should be a single whole. Many early critics, however, received it as a *group of poems* called *The Waste Land*. Eliot was so housewifely a poet that he never threw away left-overs but clearly reworked old poems as part of the process of composing new. This volume will prove a quarry for those interested in tracing the embryo of *The Hollow Men*, especially of the 'Eyes I dare not meet in dreams'.

We know how Eliot hated what he called in 1924, in his very revealing preface to Paul Valéry's *Le Serpent*, the Anglo-Saxon habit of lascivious peering between lines for biographical confession, but there is one important way in which the new biographical details about his personal distress and nervous collapse affect the poem. They demonstrate the need Eliot had at this period for help and encouragement in pulling into shape a poem too close perhaps to the events and feelings that generated it for its author to stand back judiciously and pull the threads together. It was Eliot the artist as well as the man who was exhausted. The weakness of the verse in the poor parts of discarded passages like the notorious false opening to *The Burial of the Dead*, ('He do the police in different voices—I') and the long passage in imitation of Pope may make the idolatrous uncomfortable and the detractors smug. More importantly, they should emphasise that element in the poem which belongs to the movement of European, avant-garde experimentation—conscious

[34] Quite the best scholarly and critical account of the drafts yet to appear is A. D. Moody, 'Broken Images/Voices Singing', *The Cambridge Quarterly*, VI, No. 1 (1972), 45–58.

experiment in voice,[35] idiom and style, not excluding parody and
pastiche, and the placing of Wagnerian and ragtime echoes† side by side
in a single work. Pound controlled the amount of parody and pastiche
in the final text, but it remains an essential ingredient. In fact, it was
Eliot himself who cancelled the long downtown, Americans-on-the-
loose-in-London episode; it was struck through before Pound read it.

It is remarkable too that substantial parts of the received text, often
its great moments like the April opening, the desert, the hyacinth garden,
Madame Sosostris, the unreal city and much of *What the Thunder Said*,
seem to have flowed almost unchecked, needing very little correction
by Pound. It is in such passages as these that Eliot most often ignores
Pound's suggestions or defends his own position. If, for example,
Pound's marking of 'forgetful' 'I could not speak' and 'there you feel
free' implied unease, it was ineffective since Eliot retained all three. It
is also such passages that may well bear witness to Eliot's general belief
that the subconscious plays a considerable part in composition. Given
the context of nervous illness and recuperation, one remembers his later
remark in the essay 'The *Pensées* of Pascal' (1931):

> It is a commonplace that some forms of are illness extremely favour-
> able . . . to artistic and literary composition. A piece of writing
> meditated apparently without progress for months or years, may
> suddenly take shape or word; and in this state long passages may be
> produced which require little or no retouch.

It may be that those passages of *The Waste Land* which gave the *midwife*
least trouble, and are most memorable to readers, were one of the few
compensations for a period of strain whose beginning Eliot himself
described in a letter of August 21, 1916, just over a year after his marriage,
as 'the most awful nightmare of anxiety that the mind of man could
conceive'. This period was to stretch over years which Valerie Eliot,
looking back in an interview for *The Observer*, February 20, 1972, judges
to have been 'Sheer concentrated hell'.

Some readers will still want to see *The Waste Land* as Eliot's *Hamlet*,
a play which he believed 'is full of some stuff that the writer could not
drag to light, contemplate, or manipulate into art'. There may be a
temptation for such readers now to suppose that knowing better the
nature of the 'stuff' in the case of *The Waste Land*, they can better *explain*

[35] Valerie Eliot tells us not only that Eliot based his cockney idiom upon
Ellen Kellond, their housekeeper, but that he actually met and spoke
with the Marie of Part I.

the poem. The generous selection of extracts from Eliot's letters, together with information already available in the biographies of Conrad Aiken, John Quinn and Bertrand Russell, make clearer the quality of some of the emotions which sought expression and from which his personality had to *escape* in a poem he came to dismiss later as a 'wholly insignificant grouse against life; . . . a piece of rhythmical grumbling'. If we trust the tale rather than the teller, there certainly is a strong element of disgust and weariness in the poem. It has long been the origin of discomfort to its detractors who, belonging to a more robust humanist tradition, feel threatened by its pessimism. Eliot himself saw Hamlet's disgust in Shakespeare's play as in excess of the events and people that had occasioned and should therefore merit it. In particular, he felt Gertrude was too negative and vacillating a creature to focus, objectify and contain her son's passionate disgust, so, 'his disgust envelopes and exceeds her' and is afloat, unassimilated, in the text. Similarly, there will always be those who feel that the distaste with which human, especially heterosexual love is treated in *The Waste Land* is somehow dismissive, degrading and unbalanced.[36] The draft contains a line epitomising Eliot's attitude. In the apostrophe to Fresca in *The Fire Sermon* (1) is the couplet,

> For varying forms, one definition's right:
> Unreal emotions, and real appetite.

Some may find *explanation* for this perspective in new glimpses of Eliot's own marital despair, but there is danger in proceeding from this to extract one strong thread of feeling from a whole and deliver a distorted account of the whole.

For this whole does include poignant antidotes to despair, like the figure in the hyacinth garden, whether boy or girl or both, and the fishmen of *The Fire Sermon*, who, in these early drafts, were much amplified in a long sailing episode in *Death by Water* where their human frailty (drunkenness and syphilis) does not invalidate the fact that

> The sailor attentive to the charts or to the sheets,
> A concentrated will against the tempest and the tide,
> Retains, even ashore, in public bars or streets
> Something inhuman, clean and dignified.

[36] A typical example is Ian Hamilton, *The Waste Land* in *Eliot in Perspective, A Symposium*, ed. Graham Martin (London, 1970), pp. 102–11.

It is no accident that the climactic response to the third command of the thunder god fuses lover and sailor in the familiar allegorical images of steerage and sailing. There is a fine blend of expectation and missed opportunity, control and submission:

>   the boat responded
>   Gaily, to the hand expert with sail and oar.
>   The sea was calm, your heart would have responded
>   Gaily, when invited, beating obedient
>   To controlling hands.

The drafts make it clearer too that Eliot envisaged a dialogue at this crucial moment. After the 'would have responded', and before arriving at the famous unpunctuated leap from 'To controlling hands' to 'I sat upon the shore', he attempted three half-line fillings which create a less isolated scene: (1) 'You over on the shore' (2) 'I left without you' (3) 'There I leave you/Clasping empty hands I sat upon a shore'. All these suggest the broken companionship of a pair potentially united by love.

Though we know more now of the emotional and nervous storms which seek symbolic expression in Eliot's poem, it is still more important to ask whether the *Unreal City* of his vision is an 'adequate equivalent' for them than to maintain that, because the drafts contained a misogynistic piece of Juvenalian satire reminiscent of Pope's second Epistle *Of Women* in his *Moral Essays*, this poet is writing a hidden elegy for a lost love for whom he experienced a homosexual passion.

Perhaps speculation and the biographical heresy may be held in check by the example of gossipy, self-inflating anecdotes and false conclusions drawn by Robert Sencourt in· *T. S. Eliot, A Memoir* (London, 1971). The role played, not without ·mischief and laughter tinkling among teacups, of Bertrand Russell, the Mr. Apollinax of the 1916 poem, in the difficult early days of the Eliot's marriage is clearly a complicated one. The couple must have been extremely vulnerable at the point when Russell confessed, 'I can't let them alone at present'. The original line in *A Game of Chess*, 'The ivory men make company between us', was, we are told, dropped at the request of Vivien Eliot, although she had written 'Yes and wonderful' along the margin of the passage of jazz-age neuroticism in which it came. The traditional association of the intricacies of chess with moves in the game of amorous intrigue, plus the dramatic use of chess in both *Women Beware Women* (cited in Eliot's Notes) and in *The Tempest*, where Ferdinand and Miranda are discovered at chess, would be enough to account for this line. The notion of life as a deadly game is further enforced by the fact that this section was originally sub-titled *In the Cage*, making the relation of the luxurious neurotic to the withered Sybil of the epigraph more explicit. If the cancellation suggests that the resort of a couple to chess, in their state of failure to communicate, was too painful for Vivien Eliot, it could also be conjectured that Russell may be an 'ivory man' in whose hands the suffering pair felt as manipulated pawns. But this is only an oblique hint. There may well have been afternoons when, as in *Mr. Apollinax*, 'his dry and passionate talk devoured the afternoon', but nothing essential is revealed by such a possibility.

Similarly it seems disturbingly unprofessional of *The Times Literary Supplement* reviewer in the issue of December 10, 1971, to claim that, whilst it would be obscene for Valerie Eliot to disclose the secrets of Eliot's sex life (always implying that these must and do exist), it would be indispensable to know if the poet suffered from hallucinations at any time. Without taking a theoretical stand on the biographical heresy, it seems preferable to agree with Eliot's friend Joseph Chiari,[37] who replied, 'Breakdowns and love affairs . . . are no more explanations of the poem than a piece of scenery or a model is the explanation of a painting'. Or as Eliot himself put it in *The Music of Poetry* (1942), 'this may be correct embryology, but it is not the meaning'.

If we are seeking confirmation of impressions, then, rather than explanation of mysteries, it is still questionable whether the reader needs a medical certificate of Eliot's psychic condition to authenticate his responses to the hallucinatory quality of much of *What the Thunder Said*. Eliot's reference to the strangely combined 'sources', the Shackleton expedition and the mysterious appearance of Christ after His physical mortality on the road to Emmaus, suggests his interest in the effects upon the borders of consciousness of extreme physical and psychological pressures—in these typically fused cases, the rigours of exposure to the elements and the effects of traumatic loss and grief.

Again, the revival of speculation about supposed homosexual tendencies in the poet, to account for his jaundiced presentation of heterosexual relations and his Juvenalian misogyny, has put new life into stale critical battles begun in 1952 by John Peter. In a number of *Essays in Criticism* which Eliot had withdrawn, Peter imposed a whole

[37] For a sympathetic general account of the poem see Joseph Chiari, *T. S. Eliot, Poet and Dramatist* (London, 1972), pp. 56–77.

narrative biographical' interpretation upon the poem. His basic assumption, that *The Waste Land* is a disguised elegy for a male lover, the Jean Verdenal to whom Eliot had dedicated his volume of 1917, *Prufrock and Other Observations*, was worked up with considerable ingenuity. For those with a penchant for one-tracked allegory, Peter produces Jean Verdenal as 'the one clue' and reconstitutes the poem as a monologue meditation upon deprivation through the loss of the poet's love. Peter is led into feats of ingenuity about the sexual ambiguities of the protagonists. These, he claims, spring from the homosexual nature of the informing emotion. He quotes with relish the confessional line from Dante's *Purgatorio*, Canto XXVII, l. 82, spoken by Guido Guinicelli, 'nostro peccato fu ermafrodite'. Guido immediately precedes Eliot's favourite, Arnant Daniel, in this Canto of the lustful. But Peter misses perhaps the fact that there is a more than technical distinction to be made between the hermaphrodite, who, like Tiresias, can experience love not only *of* both sexes but *as* both sexes, and the homosexual, who is limited to loving only members of his own sex. It is, after all, Tiresias's perspective and point of view which Eliot explicitly invites us to share and it is Daniel, not Guinicelli, to whom Eliot specifically alludes in line 427, 'Poi s'ascose nel foco che gli affina'. The fact that both men were poets and influences upon Dante is more important than the exact nature of their fleshly sins, as is the fact that they are willingly undergoing purgatorial fires.

> Dying into a dance,
> An agony of trance,
> An agony of flame that cannot singe a sleeve.

In the original draft of *A Game of Chess*, moreover, Eliot introduced, again from Dante, *Inferno*, V, 73–5, a pair of heterosexual lovers of great fame, the youthful adulterers Paolo and Francesca. To the female speaker's repeated question

> 'What is that noise now? What is the wind doing?'

Eliot gave the man the reply,

> 'Carrying
> Away the little light dead people'

recalling Dante's souls of the lustful,

> che insieme vanno,
> e paion s'al vento esser leggieri.

Pound objected to 'little' and the whole reference was sadly dropped. For Eliot had caught the strangely moving, almost infant quality of this pair, who were clearly grouped in his mind with Tristan and Isolde, Antony and Cleopatra and Elizabeth and Leicester. But to Peter, following his single thread, the homosexual love 'intensifies the poet's revulsion against courtship and marriage'. The portraits of Lil and Lou and their boudoir counterpart are venomous because of this personal bias. This kind of simplification leads to absurdity when the Marie[38] of the opening sled episode becomes male because Marie is an obligatory man's name on the Roman Catholic continent, to doubt at least when we are reminded that St Augustine came to 'the cauldron of unholy loves' at Carthage to escape grief over the death of a dear friend, and to real danger when it suggests that the end of the poem is an attempt to transcend this faulty human by a Christian love.

The honest doubt of Eliot's own question in line 364, 'I do not know whether a man or a woman', asked of the mysterious third figure of the hallucinatory journey, makes it impossible to rest comfortably in any firm equation of this figure with Christ. Once again, no singling out of any clue can avoid distortion both of theme and of the poem's essentially complex structure.

Nevertheless this kind of battle is now being revived on the strength of two 'moments' in the drafts. In *A Game of Chess* when the nervous lady attacks her male companion with the line, 'Do you know nothing? Do you see nothing? Do you remember nothing?' Eliot originally had the reply, 'I remember/The hyacinth garden. Those are pearls that were his eyes, yes.' The three words 'The hyacinth garden' were dropped, seemingly accidentally, from the published text. Daniel Woodward[39] recorded two variants in a typescript version of the poem in 1922 that was presented to Harvard. Firstly, 'I think we *met* first in rats' alley' (115) comes in response to 'I never know what you are thinking. Think', then 'I remember/*The Hyacinth garden*. Those are pearls that were his eyes . . .' (124-5).This established more firmly an identification of the lover in the garden with Belladona's lover. Now there prevails a further argument that, since this speaker is male and since his reminiscence associates the garden with the

[38] See note 35 above.
[39] D. Woodward, 'Notes on the publishing history and text of *The Waste Land*', *Proceedings of the Bibliographical Society of America*, LVIII (1964), 219-69.

drowned *male* figure of the poem and of Shakespeare's *The Tempest*, this encounter in the hyacinth garden of Part I must have been between male lovers. The late Greek development of the Hyacinthus myth does establish the association of the flower with the 'lovely boy', mortal male beauty beloved of the gods. That Eliot, steeped in Frazer and Weston, had the earlier Hyacinth—connected with the sacrificial fertility figures of Attis and allied myths—more in mind seems likely. But G. Wilson Knight wants to link this reminiscence with earlier draft versions of the response to the first command of the thunder in Part V. There, in answer to

> 'What have we given?'

Eliot seems first to have written,

> 'My friend, my blood friend, beating in my heart,
> The awful daring of a moment's surrender.'

It is perhaps tempting to see this *surrender* as that of blood brother to blood brother as in Greek or High Renaissance love, but this is to be careless of the exact nature of Eliot's sequence of cancellations. The passage first ran,

> *Datta:* we brother, what have we given?

so that 'my friend, my blood friend' could be seen as repeated vocatives. Equally, if the 'mon semblable mon frère' of Part I has achieved its Baudelairian effect of challenging the reader not to remain outside but to realise his resemblance to the poem's bleakly inadequate human figures, this brother too could as well be directed bardically *to* the reader, just as either 'blood' or 'friend' could be read as *objects* of given. The 'we' of the following confession seems quite clearly intended to draw us in as much as to imply a pair of speakers *within* the poem. In any case Eliot dropped both 'we brother' and 'my blood friend' to the less intense but more forceful vocative,

> my friend, blood shaking my heart.

The real importance is that the only gift offered is

> The awful daring of a moment's surrender.

Such a moment may of course include love of male friends as one of its possible instances, but passion is the specific point, passion so total as to be hidden forever after and not 'to be found in our obituaries'.

It should also be remembered that Eliot himself did not hide his memories of his friend Jean Verdenal who died at Gallipoli. In *The Criterion*, XIII, p. 452, he recalled that his memory of pre-war Paris,

> is touched by a sentimental sunset, the memory of a friend coming across the Luxembourg Gardens in the late afternoon waving a branch of lilac, a friend who was later (so far as I could find out) to be buried in the mud of Gallipoli.

Clearly, in retrospect, this friendship had great romantic intensity. It also became a personified form of Eliot's Great War experience of loss of youth, reaching almost the status of symbol. In a letter of December 17, 1917, in the midst of his marital, financial and health nightmares, Eliot gives us a rare view of his sense of the war, a factor of his life not often stressed because its main biographical importance is seen to be the fact that it brought him from Germany to Oxford and led to his permanent residence in England. But, in 1917, he could say

> everyone's individual lives are so swallowed up in the one great tragedy that one almost ceases to have personal experiences or emotions.

The Webster-like juxtaposition of flowers of erotic association with images of mortality always haunted Eliot for its elegiac possibilities. It glosses for us the notorious 'cruelty' of April which Pound fixed as the opening of *The Waste Land*—a month

> breeding
> Lilacs out of the dead land, mixing *dead*
> Memory and desire.

This collocation of spring flowers of heavy scent with the psychological compound of memory and desire is habitual in Eliot. It can be traced from *Portrait of a Lady*, where, with Jamesian indirection and inhibition, the ageing, would-be amorous lady who has a bowl of lilacs in her room, asks:

> 'What life is, you who hold it in your hands;'
> (Slowly twisting the lilac stalks.)

She addresses her question to the callously self-conscious youth who remains brash, self-possessed until,

> with the smell of hyacinths across the garden
> Recalling things that other people have desired

he is somehow caught. He returns for another encounter at which his self-possession 'gutters' as he is forced to meet the discomforting thought of his possible reaction to the lady's death,

> 'Now that we talk of dying—
> And I should have the right to smile?'

Death comes into this cluster of erotic flowers, memory and desire just as it does in *The Burial of the Dead*. For this lady, as for Marie and cousin Mary in *The Family Reunion* (who Eliot wished to enter the scene from the garden with an armful of hyacinths), desire has become subsumed into memory. Again, on the turns of the penitential stair in Part III of *Ash Wednesday* this cluster is further distilled in an almost Botticellian image of fleeting sensual beauty evoked with erotic lyricism,

> Blown hair is sweet, brown hair over the mouth blown,
> Lilac and brown hair.

By this stage Eliot has no need to be explicit about memory and desire, male and female. But coming between *Portrait of a Lady* and *Ash Wednesday*, *The Waste Land* is attempting just that poise between specific particularity and achieved symbolic representation that makes any one-dimensional biographical interpretation a narrowing distortion.

Of course biography has its place. Richard Ellman, a real literary biographer, whose judicious review of the facsimile in *New York Review of Books* (December, 1971) puts the *T.L.S.* tittle-tattle to shame, called Eliot's marriage his 'dolorous stroke', an emotional and sexual maiming. This may well account for the residue of despair counterpointed with glimpses of lost Romantic possibilities of love and beauty which makes *The Waste Land* haunt and disturb its readers. Ellman rightly sees that Eliot's contemporary *theories* of literary impersonality may well have been an antidote to the fact that *in practice* he was aware that his experience was so intense that it needed special controls. He had written to Conrad Aiken on August 21, 1916: 'I have lived through material for a score of long poems in the last six months', betraying a much closer correlation betwen experience and art than careless reading of *Tradition and the Individual Talent*, with its pseudo-scientific metaphors, often suggests.

Finally, a consideration of the nature of the language in some of the discarded passages of the drafts should modify a little what appears to be the most significant *trend* in criticism of the poem in the late sixties and early seventies. It is good to be reminded that Eliot's American origins align him more firmly than has always been realised with the American tradition of Romance[40] which flowed via the key figure of Edgar Allan Poe into French Symbolism, a movement to which we know Eliot felt drawn. It is a characteristic of this movement that it employs words in new ways to imply a discontinuous universe, whereas in what might be called classical use of language, words are communicative and denote relationships and interdependency through their syntax, because there lies behind them the notion of a continuous universe and society. Pound, in Section IV of *Hugh Selwyn Mauberley* (1920), writes of

> A consciousness disjunct,
> Being but this overblotted
> Series
> Of intermittences.

It is tempting to read these lines as a prophetic description of *The Waste Land* and its language; to read the poem as no more than a set of lyric moments hurled at us like Imagist fragments for our consciousness to play with, freely inventing a syntax and set of continuities of our own. We have, too, Eliot's own gestures towards a sense of discontinuity within his text; his 'heap of broken images', his 'fragments shored' against ruins' of a civilisation which, as an American on a voyage of discovery in European culture, he may have been shocked to find more shattered by war and historically more broken by national barriers than the later champion of a revival of Christendom expected. Some sense of this, together with his own broken nervous system, gives power to the lines,

> On Margate sands
> I can connect
> Nothing with nothing

Hence perhaps, the groping towards internationalism in the poem, the confusions of nationality, 'Bin gar keine Russin, stamm' aus Litauen, echt deutsch', and the hooded hordes stumbling over plains which, in a cancelled phrase, seem to have been *Polish* though they became merely *endless*. The linguistic equivalent for this groping towards continuity or

[40] Eliot's own interest in this tradition and its relation to the French is evident in 'In memory' and 'The Hawthorne Aspect', *The Little Review*, V (August 1918, Henry James Number), pp. 44–53.

wholeness is the climactic use of Sanskrit, the root Indo-European tongue. Kenner,[41] in his latest appraisal of what he previously called 'a poem nearly anonymous', speaks of 'a romantic quest for the primitive, for early man giving tongue to impassioned communication with thunder and falling water . . . united with romantic orientalism (Xanadu) to draw the philological imagination back through Sanskrit to Indo-European roots.' That the words required a gloss ironically marks our distance from any such roots.

Nevertheless, the kind of language used even in the received text, and certainly in the drafts, is by no means uniform or consistently 'disjunct'. The drafts contain several passages using discourse and syntax in a more conventional manner than the more symbolist passages in which words appear more autonomous. They contain too a characteristic which Pound clearly disliked and which Eliot probably adopted under the influence of the eighteenth-century writers he was imitating—the use of aphoristic or clinching phrases and summarising lines which imply a universe and social order all too continuous and commonly held. Perhaps the best example is the expansion of the apostrophe to London, a passage almost Johnsonian in tone. Johnson's own *London* was a poem in imitation of the Third Satire of Juvenal and would clearly have been well known to Eliot at this period when he was himself imitating.

> London, the swarming life you kill and breed
> Huddled between the concrete and the sky
> Responsive to the momentary need
> Vibrates unconscious to its formal destiny.

The presence of such lines as these, side by side with the more 'broken' syntax and allusive moments of the poem in its draft form, should temper eagerness to describe it too sophisticatedly as modernist while not forbidding recognition of its consciously experimental nature and the symbolist characteristics which Pound wished to promote.

II

It is interesting that in his 1944 lecture 'Johnson as Critic and Poet' Eliot was to criticise Johnson's *London* for having a 'suspicion of falsity' as an 'indictment of a whole city'—a criticism frequently levelled against his own treatment of London and its highly selected people in *The Waste*

41 Hugh Kenner, *The Pound Era* (London, 1972).

Land. He puts this false, strained quality down to the fact that Johnson was not a natural satirist but a moralist given to the habit of generalisation, whereas

> what keeps the poem alive is the undercurrent of personal feeling, the bitterness of the hardships, slights, injuries and privations, really experienced by Johnson in his youth.

The parallel with the case of Eliot's poem is tempting. Moreover, one of the important things to emerge from the drafts is precisely this habit of uttering generalisations. But Eliot did not consider himself a satirist. In a letter to his brother written on February 15, 1920, following the Knopf publication of his *Poems* of 1920 he had complained that

> even here [i.e. London] I am considered by the ordinary newspaper critic as a wit or satirist, and in America I suppose I shall be thought merely disgusting.

Many have found Eliot's 'Unreal City', both commercial London, The City, and *Civitas Diaboli*—the antitype to St. Augustine's *Civitas Dei*—partial, satirically strained, just as he had found Dr. Johnson's Juvenalian satire to be. From the drafts it becomes clearer, however, that Eliot wanted this vision to be taken as grave rather than satirically distorted, and there is one important line which got sadly dropped along with the generalising apostrophe quoted above. It falls between the address to London and the violet hour that heralds the typists' and clerks' indulgence of 'Unreal emotion and real appetite'. The line, 'Not here O Glaucon, but in another world', reminds us of the alternative to the Unreal City, the Real *Civitas Dei*. As Valerie Eliot notes, Adeimantus and Glaucon, brothers in Plato, were speakers in *The Republic*. She conjectures that Eliot was alluding to Book IX, 592 A–B, to a passage which inspired the Stoics and Christians, and especially St. Augustine, as it contains the idea of a pattern or *form* of a city laid up in heaven for contemplation; a pattern never to be found or realised on earth. The falling towers of

> Jerusalem Athens Alexandria
> Vienna London
> Unreal

are unreal in this Platonic sense, not merely in the sense of being hallucinatory and dream-like in their poetic presentation. The higher reality, against which the Unreal City and its unlovely and unloving people are measured and found wanting, was thus given a fleeting and oblique mention in the original.

Similarly, the arguments that have raged over whether God is in any way present in *The Waste Land*, a poem of Eliot's pre-conversion days, will be reopened over the fact that in the long, often callowly phrased shipwreck passage in *Death by Water*, there is an oblique reference to the deity as 'Another'. This section, now the shortest in the poem, and in many respects a reworking of lines in the earlier French poem *Dans le restaurant*, was originally of 93 lines and included a shipwreck off The Dry Salvages. It is modelled upon Ulysses' wreck in Dante's *Inferno*, Canto XXVI, with side-glances at Tennyson's *Ulysses*. In comparing Dante and Tennyson in their treatment of the Ulysses of whom Homer wrote,

> He saw the cities and knew the thoughts of many men
> And suffered many sorrows in his heart upon the sea.

Eliot said that, whereas 'Dante is telling a story, Tennyson is only stating an elegiac mood'. Eliot's clumsiness in handling his seaman's idiom makes it hard to determine which he is attempting. The mode is narrative at first and the 'I', rather like Coleridge's Ancient Mariner, stands apart from the crew—involved in the action yet reminiscent. The voyage begins in 'kingfisher weather' and the 'garboard strake' leaks as it is to do much later in the poem *Marina*. The sailors, obviously to be linked with fishmen of *The Fire Sermon*, laugh and recall the 'pleasant violin' of 'Marm Brown's joint'. The narrator 'laughs not', but hears the sirens' song that 'charmed my senses', echoing both *The Tempest* and the 'drowning of the senses' in the boudoir of *A Game of Chess*. The ship (it is possible Eliot had the *Titanic* in mind) crashes into an iceberg as Dante had Ulysses' ship caught and whirled round approaching a brown mountain. A powerful phrase at this point recalls Conrad's 'The horror! The horror!' which was Eliot's original epigraph to *The Waste Land*:

> no one dared
> To look into another's face, or speak
> In the horror of the illimitable scream
> Of a whole world about us.

This echoes too the differently motivated speechlessness of the lover in the hyacinth garden, just as the mariner's final 'Remember me' links with *la Pia* whose lines in *Purgatorio*, V. 133

'Ricorditi di me, che son la Pia;
'Siena mi fe', disfecemi Marema'

Eliot quoted in his Notes. It may also recall Dido's plangently repeated
lament, in Purcell's *Dido and Aeneas*, 'Remember me', uttered before
her suicide. Eliot attempts a switch of idioms here which, for me, fails
lamentably. He modulates from

'Home and mother
Where's a cocktail shaker'

grimly braving the ice with the humour of despair, to

'Remember me
And if Another knows, I know I know not'

which recalls 'and I knew nothing' in the hyacinth garden episode.
This mention of God is, of course, agnostic, but its very tentativeness
makes it lyrically quite powerful. But this episode was to go, and those
who would make the whole poem an elegy on a drowned male lover
should note well that it was Pound who had to persuade Eliot to retain
the Phlebas passage to ten lines which forms *Death by Water* in the
received text.

Another of these fleeting glimpses of something *positive* though un-
attained linking knowledge with spiritual insight was thrown into relief
by the poem's original epigraph, the whole interrogatory paragraph
from Conrad's *Heart of Darkness* culminating in the famous 'The
horror—the horror'. Pound felt that Conrad did not merit such a
position; but though Eliot accepted Pound's view, he did maintain of
the quotation that 'It is much the most appropriate I can find, and somewhat elucidative'. The passage ran,

Did he live his life again in every detail of desire, temptation, and
surrender during that supreme moment of complete knowledge? He
cried in a whisper at some image, at some vision,—cried out twice, a
cry that was no more than a breath—'The horror! The horror'.

There would be much to be said for adding this to the received text of
Eliot's poem for it is, indeed, somewhat elucidative.

It throws into sharper relief a hint that was always there, of a deliberate
contrasting of the transcendent moment, whether erotic or spiritual, in
the hyacinth garden, where the quester lover declares

> I was neither
> Living nor dead, and I knew nothing
> Looking into the heart of light, the silence.

and Kurtz's famous pronouncement from 'the heart of darkness' where he feels he has achieved total knowledge. The pronouncement, which Marlow the narrator admires because it is a judgement, is uttered before death but at a point where Kurtz too cannot be said to be alive, save medically. What is even more elucidative is the hint this quotation gives of what Eliot's method and poetic stance or *point of view* are to be in the poem. Like that of the Sybil in her cage who replaced him, Kurtz is in a state of suspended animation, delivering utterances from, in his case, a frantic wisdom springing out of a total vision of desire, temptation and self-surrender. The utterances are no more than whispers, scarcely audible, just as the Sibyl's riddles are scattered and require solving. It may well be that Eliot felt his poem to be a set of whispers uttered out of a related sense of self-revelation under extreme pressure.

Finally, there is a small detail in the drafts which happily counteracts the doubts which may be roused by the weakest parts. It comes in what has always been recognised as a moment of special resonance in the final text. It also shows Eliot at work as his own editor, rather than in collaboration with Pound. In the original of *The Fire Sermon*, Eliot had his apostrophe to The City following a much longer version of the typist episode, which was arranged in a b a b quatrains. Pound complained that this metre was a mix-up of the Augustan couplet, still ringing in Eliot's ears after his attempt to recreate Pope in a passage on Fresca's toilette, and 'grishkin', i.e. the stanzaic period of *Poems—1920*, including *Mr. Eliot's Sunday Morning Service* and *Sweeney Among the Nightingales*. The division of this passage into stanzas does lead to facile, over-insistent rhymes and its diffuseness leads to attempts at social-realism which Pound, a longer resident in London, detects as false notes. The poor clerk's scurf rhymes all too patly with 'turf' and the typist has a Japanese print bought in Oxford Street. 'Not in *that* lodging house', cringes Pound.

Eliot accepted all this and tightened things up and abandoned the stanza as a unit. But he had already ignored Pound's objection to Blakeian allegorisation of London in Part I[42] and now continues it, journeying

---

[42] For a suggestive account of the poem's topography see Robert A. Day, 'The City Man in *The Waste Land*', *P.M.L.A.*, LXXX (1965), pp. 285–91.

> There where the tower was traced against the night
> Of Michael Paternoster Royal, red and white.

This is, in two senses, well on the way to the lovely lines,

> where the walls
> Of Magnus Martyr hold
> Inexplicable splendour of Ionian white and gold

but the tentative and architecturally wobbly middle stage reveals a fascinating moment of synaesthesia,

> there the walls
> Of Magnus Martyr stood, and stand, and hold

1. Inviolable
2. Their joyful splendour of Corinthian white and gold
3. Inexplicable.

The word 'inviolable' had of course been used in *A Game of Chess*, of the voice of the rudely forced nightingale. Pound had marked it *there* as too 'penty', presumably feeling that as a word and as a rhythmical unit it made the line too much of a traditional pentameter. But Eliot retained it there. Now it slips in again, suggesting not merely carelessness, but the possibility that the idea of inviolability, even among falling towers (Eliot was always a champion of schemes to restore and preserve the City churches) was really in his mind. The fishmen and their locale of public bar and a church, St. Magnus Martyr, traditionally associated with the sea. *are* inviolable. St. Magnus, a Norseman and sea-rover, escaped his pagan persecutors by jumping into the sea and this church, like the Grail chapel itself, is near water on the river bank. Just as the 'heart of light' is more explicitly contrasted with 'heart of darkness' in the drafts, so here 'inviolable splendour' makes more forceful the contrast between the fishmen's church of St. Magnus and the bankers' church, St. Mary Woolnoth, which is across Lombard Street from Lloyds Bank. The banker-poet wryly reminds us of this latter association in *The Burial of the Dead*, where

> Saint Mary Woolnoth kept the hours
> With a dead sound on the final stroke of nine

a very 'real' detail in his Platonically unreal city. It is such moments in his drafts that confirm a sense, always there in *The Waste Land*, that, for all the horror of mundane unreality, there are also fleeting glimpses of what was to develop into the moment in *Burnt Norton* where the surface of a dry concrete pool

> was filled with water out of sunlight

and

> The surface glittered out of heart of light.

List of Eliot's Critical Essays mentioned in the text

'Thoughts after Lambeth', first published 1931. See *Selected Essays* (London, 1961), pp. 363–87 [p. 7].

'Tradition and the Individual Talent', first published in *The Egoist*, VI, iv, v (1919). See *Selected Essays* (London, 1961), pp. 13–22 [pp. 8, 9, 46, 48].

'The Metaphysical Poets', first published in *Times Literary Supplement* (Oct. 20th, 1921). See *Selected Essays* (London, 1961), pp. 281–91 [pp. 9, 49].

'Ulysses, Order and Myth', *The Dial* (1923), pp. 480–83.

'Essay on Massinger,' first published in *Times Literary Supplement* (Nov. 18th, 1926). See *Selected Essays* (London, 1961), pp. 205–20 [p. 46].

The Use of Poetry and the Use of Criticism, first published in 1933 (London, Faber & Faber) [pp. 48, 51].

'The Frontiers of Criticism', first delivered as a lecture at the University of Minnesota, 1956. See *On Poetry and Poets* (London, 1961), pp. 103–18 [pp. 47, 49].

'The Music of Poetry', first published in Glasgow, 1942. See *On Poetry and Poets* (London, 1961), pp. 26–38 [p. 52].